"Everyone has a HERO lo[...] [...]s of their mind...when you [...] will skyrocket you to prev[...]. As your eyes travel from on[...] [...]ext, you will suddenly become aware of the masterful job Sharif has done in guiding you to this special place. I love it, so will you."

— **Bob Proctor, Chairman,**
Life Success Productions;
Author, *You Were Born Rich*.

"Sharif will inspire you to become a better leader and pursue excellence for life."

— **Chris Ridabock, CEO,**
J.J. Barnicke Ltd.,
and former Chair,
Toronto Board of Trade

"Touches all the senses that inspire and motivate us to become more...A great read, well researched, and very inspiring."

— **John Watt, President and**
Senior Creative Director,
Megawatt Ideas

"There comes a point where the visionary leader makes the decision to sacrifice all else for the vision. That is the point at which the visionary becomes a hero. For those heroes this book will bring perspective and inspiration."

— **Baldo B. Minaudo, President**
MetroActive Lifestyle Network

The dreams of the whispering wind
enter my heart
and permeate my soul
to tell of a tale untold
yet fully known and once traversed
bringing me back to the place I cry for
in all my wandering days on earth.

To Paula,

onwards and upwards !

PSYCHOLOGY
OF THE
HERO SOUL

SHARIF N. KHAN

Copyright © 2004 by Sharif N. Khan

All rights reserved. No part of this book may be reproduced or transmitted in any form or by any means, electronic or mechanical, including photocopying, recording, or by any information storage and retrieval system, without permission in writing from the publisher.

Published by Diamond Mind Publishing
35 Douville Court, Toronto, Ontario M5A 4E7
Canada
416-417-1259

Printed in Canada

Cover Design by Pablo Viola

ISBN 0-9731922-0-8

First Paperback Edition

Most Diamond Mind Books are available at special quantity discounts for bulk purchases for sales promotions, premiums, fund-raising, or educational use. Special books or book excerpts can also be created to fit specific needs.

For details, contact: Diamond Mind Publishing, 35 Douville Court, Toronto, Ontario M5A 4E7; (416) 417-1259

DEDICATION

I dedicate this book to E. Jim G. Ross, founder of the Canadian Academy of Method Acting. Mr. Ross has committed his entire life to promoting heroes and teaching people to endlessly pursue excellence. He is my teacher, mentor, and major source of inspiration in my creative work. Mr. Ross is one of those unsung heroes we all wish we knew. Thank you, Jim, for giving me the gift of knowledge and wonder.

CONTENTS

ABOUT THE AUTHOR

As President of Diamond Mind Enterprises, an organization devoted to helping people awaken their inner potential to live their highest life, Sharif Khan has dedicated over ten years research in the field of human development and studying great leaders. His vision is to inspire the world and make a positive difference in people's lives.

A dynamic and highly engaging professional speaker and workshop facilitator, Sharif provides inspirational keynotes and leadership development seminars that entertain, educate, and empower. His unique approach focuses on developing each participant's hero potential.

To learn more about the author, please visit:
www.herosoul.com

ACKNOWLEDGEMENTS

An idea that's time has come is a force unstoppable. The whole universe cooperates to bring about its fruition. I am just a vehicle for its creation. For the people who have come into my life, you are part of this grand scheme, and I express my undying gratitude:

To my mother, Shama, for your unconditional love and support, and for putting up with me all these years. Thanks Mom, for being the light in my life.

To my two wonderful brothers and best friends, Junaid and Fareed, who have always been there for me.

To my father, Dr. Nasim, who is smiling down on me. Your belief and faith in me since I was a kid is a flame that grows brighter in my heart.

To David Robson for being my friend, believing in me, and being a mentor. You have taught me the art of business, and in many ways, the art of life. Thank you.

To Lisa Cherniak, Executive Director of Artists Against Racism, for editing my first draft and for supporting a truly worthy cause.

To Rebecca Rosenblat for your inspiration, friendship, and love. I am forever grateful for your years of encouragement and gentle guidance.

To Peter Vybihal for pursuing excellence in the craft of writing as an art and having a profound effect on my writing profession.

To Khalid Bokhari for your undying friendship and for being like a father to me.

To Tony Meers for your continued support at SGI.

To Roger Pierce for embracing the message in my book and your help in connecting me to the right people.

To Peter Lessmann for living with integrity and upholding decent values.

To my beloved readers who want to *know*, who strive for more, who strive for excellence. Without you, my work is an empty vessel.

I would also like to humbly thank the many people who have given generously of their time, support, and teachings: Harold Harder, Trevor Brown, Lynn Manwar, Rick Okada, Iqbal Siddiqui, Wayne MacPhail, Matt Adamson, John Watt, John Cruz, James Buffin, James Sinclair, Jim Healey, Ayo Bankole, Winston Lau, Kim Whalen, Lynne Hussey, Danish Ahmed, Baldo, Dominik Loncar, Sheryl Rogers, Mini, Pablo, Ajay Dhebar, Nathalie-Roze Fischer, Leslie Till, Scott Armstrong, Leigh Anne Pearson, Scott Macintosh, Ned Ma, Andres and Hose Bustos, Alex and Flor Hurtado, Les Brown, Mark Victor Hansen, David Chilton, Brian and Bob Proctor, Peter Urs Bender, Robin Sharma, Debbie Ford, Joseph Campbell, Steven K. Scott, and Chris Ridabock Sr.

Finally, above all, I want to thank God. Through faith the impossible is made possible. You have given me hope, and courage, and the will to go on despite the odds. You have inspired me to give the best of my best, and beyond. You have given me the power of love. Thank you for blessing me with a gift, a vision that I can share with the rest of humanity.

A WORD FROM THE AUTHOR
What This Book Can Do for You

This book will inspire you to awaken and illuminate the hero soul within, rekindling your passion for greatness. There is a superman and superwoman that lies dormant in everyone of us. The purpose of this book is to get you to deeply connect with this power. By touching all your senses and stirring the emotions, a chord in your soul will be strummed, and a hero will rise within.

If this seems like a very bold statement to you, it is. It will require you to embrace change and challenge yourself like you've never done before. Change is not easy. If it were easy, you would not learn anything new because it is stuff you already know and find cozy. Einstein said it best, "The problems that exist in the world today cannot be solved by the level of thinking that created them." Applying this to yourself, if you keep thinking in the same way, you will remain at the same level and keep getting the same results.

If you read this book thoughtfully, with an open mind, you too can experience the euphoria that comes from inspiration and expansion of soul. By abandoning the status quo, you liberate your mind to experience a new life with new power. The moment you decide to make changes in your life, is the moment when you experience true freedom.

You may find this book to be a very rewarding challenge. What makes this book unique is its multidisciplinary approach to the concept of hero. It is a composite of the universal hero that is all-encompassing: involving ideas from human potential development, religion, mythology, philosophy, the arts, spirituality, and psychology. (Although Webster's dictionary defines psychology as "the science of mind and behavior," its original definition is the study of the *psyche,* which is the Greek root word meaning breath, life, or the invisible animating force called Spirit. Both the cognitive and spiritual aspects of the human machine need to be studied for a complete picture).

Because of this book's integrative, holistic approach, the no-nonsense executive who has a focus on professional development will be wondering what spirituality has to do with leadership. A person of one religious faith may find it difficult to understand the viewpoint of another faith. Creative types may only be interested in the dramatic arts and mythology aspects of the hero.

My argument here is that one cannot fully understand and intimately connect with a subject matter unless he or she studies all aspects of it. His Holiness the Dalai Lama, in his recent book, *An Open Heart*, states, "The more you explore a topic and subject it to mental scrutiny, the more profoundly you understand it." By studying all aspects of the hero soul you can become a multidimensional leader: a person of rich character, substance, breadth, and scope. The art of cultivating the hero soul requires discernment, depth of character, a certain level of sophistication, and a high degree of awareness, self-knowledge, and self-acceptance.

This advanced concept of what I call the 'Renaissance Hero' has evolved into a being that is in tune with the noble values of the soul. The hero or leader of today operates from wisdom, compassion, and caring. Love, not greed, is the central, operating force. The 'command and control' ideology of the old-style leadership is collapsing and giving way to a de-centralized, more autonomous leadership where every member of the team is his or her own leader in today's service and information economy.

Why choose this path? Because the old-style leadership that tries so hard to control causes too much stress, illness, and depression in the person trying to control, as well as the people being controlled. The new hero, the new leader, operates from authentic power. Authentic power is power that is in harmony with nature. It comes from being in tune with your soul and allows you to effortlessly achieve.

When you have authentic power, people will naturally seek your leadership, because you inspire them to be their own leaders. You won't need to insult their intelligence by using the latest 'motivational' techniques to manipulate. They will feel self-empowered and inspired. This more enlightened form of leadership will provide you and your associates with wholeness, balance, and meaning in the workplace and in life.

In order to accomplish this, you must abandon the old ways of thinking and embrace the new. There is much resistance to change in society. A certain comfort level exists with our current ways of thinking. When you feel resistance to a new idea, be your own leader and ask yourself, "Will allowing myself to change cause a breakthrough in my thinking, and ultimately in my life?" If the answer is 'yes,' great. If the answer is 'no,' then move on to the next concept. Use what works for you, and throw out the rest. But choose carefully, because your current thinking determines your future.

This book is designed to touch all the senses and subtly invoke hidden powers that you never thought you had. Some of the more dramatic, poetics in the book will initiate learning at a deeper, subconscious level when you don't even realize you are learning. By embracing the new psychology, the psychology of the hero soul, you won't have to chase after success and rewards. You will have authentic power. Success and rewards will come to you.

All beauty inspires transformation. When you are ready to embrace change and look deeply at the beauty of your soul, you will experience amazing improvement in yourself. This will enable you to lead a victorious life.

These leadership principles of the hero soul apply just as much to the boardroom as the bedroom. Everyone can strive to be a hero, whether it's in the workplace, in the family, or among friends. Wanting to become a better husband or wife, a better father or mother, a better brother or sister, is just as noble as wanting to be a heroic figure in business, politics, religion, entertainment, or sports. Everyone plays a leadership role in his or her time.

For those that are ready to take the path of herohood, I salute you. Be prepared for substantive transformation and renewal. My hope is to inspire you to reach new heights of achievement that you never dared before. The great Helen Keller once stated, "One can never consent to creep when one feels the impulse to soar." May this book spark that impulse inside you to soar.

INTRODUCTION

"But though towards the end of the battle the men felt all
the horror of what they were doing, though they would have
been glad to leave off, some incomprehensible, mysterious
power continued to control them, and they still brought up
the charges, loaded, aimed and applied the match, though
only one artilleryman survived out of every three, and
though they stumbled and panted with fatigue, perspiring
and stained with blood and powder. The cannon-balls flew
just as swiftly and cruelly from both sides, crushing human
bodies, and that terrible work, which was not done by the
will of man, but at the will of Him who governs men and
worlds, continued."
   – excerpt from Tolstoy's, *War and Peace*

This book started off as a mini research project to help me
create a heroic protagonist in my work of fiction that
would be unforgettable – a colossal figure, largess
universal as the sun. I wanted to deliver to my audience a
little moment of truth in my fictional character that would
be memorable. But in my obsession to capture the truth, I
could not stop, even though I would have been relieved to
do so. I was possessed by a vision that would not leave
me, and haunted by a force I could not for the life of me
control.

There is a flashback scene in the second part of *The
Godfather* where Michael Corleone, who ironically ends
up taking his father's place as the Don, looks back on his
life: returning home fresh out of college, he tells his
shocked family that he has enlisted in the army, not
wanting any part of the Mafia underworld, only to become
what was destined in his blood. In the same way, I looked
back after having finished this book, wanting originally
only to have written a couple days of private notes, and

ending up taking over a year compiling and synthesizing years of research from several sources, and then extracting only the essence of what makes a hero, to present to a very public audience. Unlike the Don, however, I looked back with a sense of delight and pure joy at the work that unfolded.

My original motivation had been to create a hero that had the capacity to overcome limiting beliefs and undergo a powerful transformative and renewing experience. This is because I wanted to learn how to break free from my own bonds: the chains of racism and prejudice.

The events of our childhood forcefully shape our lives whether we are conscious of it or not. The victimization of racism that I faced when I was young, led me on a lifetime quest to understand how one overcomes adversity, how one maintains a positive concept of self, and how world leaders triumph over the bonds of ignorance to achieve liberation of mind.

I combined this knowledge with my extensive studies of the inner makings of heroes around the world for the development of the main character in my story. By going deeper and deeper into my topic, it suddenly dawned on me that I was still trapped in my ego. Ego is about ME! ME! ME! The soul is about WE. It wasn't about me. It was about the entire human race. Instead of selfishly hoarding knowledge, why not share it with the rest of the world? The knowledge that I acquired over the years helped me enormously in all areas of my life. Being my own worst critic, I believed that if it helped me, sharing this knowledge would also help others. From then on, my work became a public endeavor.

As my work progressed, I gained an even deeper understanding of my subject matter. It became very apparent to me that great leaders were in short supply. I realized the world lacks true heroes because people lack courage. We live in a wimpy world. We live in an age of constant fear. People are afraid. Many fear death, and many more fear life. Few people have the courage to show their true passion. Even fewer are willing to take a stand for a cause. Many pseudo leaders don't do what they say they are going to do because they have no honor or integrity. Their soul is asleep.

Corporations, today, have lost touch with the human soul. Profit is King while people its slave, instead of the other way around. People are just expense reports and nothing more. There is not enough compassion in the workplace. The soul has been taken away. There is no loyalty, no honor, and no respect. Only low morale, mistrust, and growing resentment towards those who control but do not lead.

I believe that the time has come to put the soul back into the corporation. And it is the responsibility of every political, business, and religious leader to work hand in hand to ensure this happens by promoting heroes in the workplace and in every day life. Heroes that are in tune with the nobility of the soul.

We must tune with our souls and re-connect with our higher Self to become great again. This theme, this 'incomprehensible, mysterious power' that Leo Tolstoy spoke of, took hold of me and propelled me to experience ever expanding spheres of knowledge. I learned that being a large-souled hero means living by principles that are eternal: hope, faith, integrity, respect, honor, duty, courage, strength, sacrifice, excellence, humility, contentment, serenity, patience, generosity, wisdom, compassion, caring, and the greatest of them all – love.

By studying and immersing myself in these principles, I became inspired. In my inspiration, I was overtaken by a vision. Instead of beckoning the muse, the muse came and beckoned me. My vision was to inspire the world with these spiritual values. I became consumed by this vision every waking day. And the days and nights blurred together. Everything seemed like a surreal dream. My project had become much larger than myself.

On September 11, 2001, as I was finishing my first draft, the world changed forever when terrorists destroyed the New York World Trade Center and bombed the Pentagon with hijacked U.S. airliners. Thousands of innocent civilian lives were lost as the world looked on in horror and disbelief. I then realized why I was so consumed by this vision. I realized that I was simply acting as a conduit for divine expression. That it was my duty to communicate a vision that will awaken our collective soul. For such horrors can only happen if there is no soul, and only ego in its stead.

Would understanding this stop terrorism and war? No. For the cycles of world creation and world destruction will eventually play their course, just as death is the inevitable consequence of life. But it is in how we choose to live, and how we meet our death that will make all the difference in the world.

May this book inspire you to choose to live with passion and greatness every waking day, and to meet every challenge with wisdom and courage. I believe that the indomitable strength of the human spirit will shine through, if we let it. And upon doing so, we fly.

BREAK ON THROUGH TO THE OTHER SIDE

"There is the known, and there is the unknown, and in between is the doors."
– Jim Morrison

"Break on through to the other side...Where the day destroys the night and night divides the day...Break on through to the other side." These were the famous haunting words sung by the American poet, rock artist, Jim Morrison of *The Doors*. With these words, he electrified an entire generation. And with these words, he began his own destruction. Morrison was talking about the great hero quest that he longed to take: to break on through to the other side, the dark side, the spiritual side, the unknown, and beyond. To penetrate the deepest darkness of his soul, enter on to the other side of pure light, and return with a vision to heal himself and his people. But Jim Morrison never returned from the dark side.

Jim was not prepared to enter into the dark side. He did not understand the psychology of the hero soul, and did not have the capacity to deal with the horror of his inner demons. Instead of slaying the dragon, his ego, he fed his ego with more fire and hatred. He set out to kiss the serpent, to ride the snake to the end of time and beginning of eternity, but he was swallowed by it. He was consumed by his own darkness.

The same thing happened with Jimi Hendrix and Janis Joplin. They got stuck in the dark side. By using artificial means, massive quantities of drugs and alcohol, they were able to shut the spinning wheels of their mind and receive a small glimpse of the other side. In their drug-induced trances, they caught the occasional beams of light on 'the other side' that penetrated their darkness with visions of poetic expression. But they did so at a great cost to themselves and people around them. These visions may have electrified their generation, but they did not heal. They simply entertained people, and at best, during their peak, may have satisfied a small yearning inside. But their music did not elevate people to a higher level of understanding like Mozart, Beethoven, or John Lennon.

Joseph Campbell, in his book, *The Hero with a Thousand Faces,* beautifully illustrates the path of the hero: "the birth, life, and death of the individual may be regarded as a descent into unconsciousness and return. The hero is the one who, while still alive, knows and represents the claims of the superconsciousness which throughout creation is...unconscious. The adventure of the hero represents the moment when, while still alive, he found and opened the road to the light beyond the dark walls of our living death."

The penultimate hero is able to enter into the unconscious realm and beyond, still awake, and bring back the boons that elevate entire civilizations and create the titan works that give birth to cultural enlightenment. He or she has the strength, will, courage, and inner capacity to defeat the dark demons of the other side. Heroes also survive the cruel impact of the world. They learn to effectively deal with the initial, furious scorn and ridicule from people that don't understand them upon their return. They learn to shatter the ego, and return transformed, offering people the life elixir to renew and transform themselves as well. They cause the illumination of the collective soul and liberation of the mind. The highest purpose of the hero is to provide a vision that heals our tribe called humanity.

Can we all aspire to become like this in our lifetime? This is a question that I cannot answer, because I have no authority to decide what is possible and what is not. The important thing to remember is that this work is a composite of the universal hero in a state of perfection. We only need to access a small fraction of this power to experience a new life with new power and new blood.

REBEL WITH A CAUSE

"If a man hasn't discovered something that he will die for, he isn't fit to live."
– Martin Luther King, Jr.

Heroes are rebels with a cause. Rebels because they challenge the traditional ways of thinking and refuse to follow the herd. When naysayers challenge them by saying something can't be done, they rebel, and prove them wrong. They are leaders, not followers. Real leaders have such a strong conviction in what they are doing that they continue to lead even if no one is willing to follow.

Pseudo leaders, on the other hand, need applause desperately. They cannot operate without followers. At the extreme end of the spectrum, Hitler, Franco, Mussolini, Stalin, Pol Pot, were all pseudo leaders. They were not leaders; they were extremely insecure people who gave in to the power of the dark side. Some people believe that they were great leaders because they had a tremendous following. This is a dangerously deceptive assumption. One can be their own leader, and does not necessarily need a following for the sake of having followers. If this were not the case, then David Koresh and Jim Jones could be called leaders instead of the false prophets that they were.

These fake leaders horde knowledge and control people with fear. Their chief aim is to achieve absolute power over others for their own personal gain. Real leaders share their knowledge. They teach people to be their own leaders. They lead by example and operate from a deep sense of wisdom, compassion, and caring. They have a higher cause to educate and liberate. Heroes are rebels *with* a cause.

Death is the crown of the hero soul. The true hero is prepared to die for what they believe in. They fight for a worthy cause, for a principle much larger than themselves. They fight for all of humanity. Nelson Mandela, the most honored hero of our time, a man who fought all his life for justice and equality, a man who endured 27 years of hardship in the prisons of South Africa, said this about his rebellion against apartheid:

"During my lifetime I have dedicated myself to this struggle of the African people. I have fought against white domination, and I have fought against black domination. I have cherished the ideal of a democratic and free society in which all persons live together in harmony and with equal opportunities. It is an ideal which I hope to live for and to achieve. But if needs be, it is an ideal for which I am prepared to die." [Taken from his autobiography, *Long Walk to Freedom.*]

Here was a great man who stood up for what he believed in. He defied the white-dominated, apartheid government of South Africa. And when they tried with all their might to break him, he would not break. He only grew stronger. And finally, with awesome power, he rose to topple the apartheid system of oppression to become the first black President of South Africa!

Terry Fox is another most beautiful rebel hero who will be remembered forever. His story is about his personal rebellion against giving up in the face of the ugly cancer that was destroying his life. At eighteen, he lost his leg due to bone cancer that was threatening to spread throughout his body. Instead of giving up like most people, he rebelled against the norms of 'disability' and even against himself. Heroes are intelligent rebels who rebel even against their own perceived mediocrity.

Terry Fox decided to run straight across Canada with a prosthetic leg to raise funds for cancer research. He defied convention, and turned his 'tragedy' into triumph. After over a year of grueling training, Terry Fox set off to run across Canada, and ran for 143 days. He ran two thirds across Canada before losing his life to cancer. Terry might have lost his battle against cancer, but he won the war by gaining the inspiration of millions of people around the world. Terry lost his life to cancer, but his cause was much greater than his own life. In the end, Terry raised $24.2 million dollars for cancer research. After his death, people from all across the globe still partake in the annual Terry Fox Run to continue to raise funds to fight cancer. Because Terry was a rebel with a cause, his legacy lives on.

SACRIFICE

"Great achievement is usually born of great sacrifice, and is never the result of selfishness."
– Napoleon Hill

The surface definition of sacrifice means to give up something of value now to gain something even more valuable in the future. It inherently implies 'giving something up' or doing a distasteful chore. Heroes penetrate deeper into the far more substantive meaning hidden in the language. The meaning of the Latin derivative of the word sacrifice is 'sacred office,' which means to hold one's work or mission sacred - dear to one's heart. Something sacred is something beloved to our hearts. Anything sacred requires deep reverence and respect. It is holy and divine.

From this higher perspective, the whole meaning of sacrifice changes dramatically. Doing one's best, overcoming great struggle, enduring hardships, no longer are chores for the hero soul. They are labors of love for something they hold dear and divine.

Why did Robert De Niro endure such strain in the filming of *The Raging Bull* by sparring hundreds of rounds with the real boxing champion, Jake La Motta, and gaining 50 pounds to prepare for his role? Why does Tiger Woods practice over six hours a day on his game covering the technical, mental and physical weight-training aspects? Why did Michael Jordan play the '97 Championship Game against the Utah Jazz with the flu and a 102 degree temperature and still come out winning the Championship and the MVP trophy? Why did John Grisham, now one of the highest paid authors in history, get up at 5:00 a.m. every morning for three years to write his first book,

A Time to Kill, only to be rejected numerous times before finally getting published by a small publishing house? The answer: SACRIFICE!

What makes these heroes great is their ability to sacrifice. They hold their work sacred. And that means having an enormous respect for their audience, for their customers, for their coworkers, and for their profession. It means giving the best of the best of the best. It means not being satisfied until it is just right. Always striving for perfection. Always being conscious of how they impact other people's lives as role models. Always looking to give back to humanity a little moment of truth. Delivering a performance that is unforgettable every time.

There are higher and higher degrees of sacrifice as with any universal principle. Self-sacrifice for the sole benefit of humanity is the highest form of sacrifice. There is the more literal aspect of this heroic sacrifice as in the case of the brave police officers, firefighters, ambulance and medical crew members, and ordinary civilians, who risked their lives to save others from the very cowardly terrorist attacks on the New York World Trade Center. We can also experience this aspect in the mother who runs into a burning building and summons superhuman strength to lift a slab of heavy concrete to save her child.

Then we have the everyday working heroes who get up every morning to feed, clothe, and provide for their children whether they feel like it or not. These people are the light bearers for our future generations. I was watching Larry King one day on CNN interviewing Dean Cain, the host of the television series *Ripley's Believe It Or Not*. In the interview, Dean played a video clip from his show that really grabbed my attention: a young mother, with no arms, was changing the diapers and feeding and caring for her newborn baby, with only her feet.

I was astonished. I couldn't do what she was doing with my arms! She was doing everything from taking care of her baby, to the household chores, and even driving with only her feet. As I was watching this beautiful mother gently caressing her new born baby with her feet, a wave of loving emotion hit me and spread throughout my body and deep into my soul. I wanted to transport myself through the television set and into this mother's life – wanting simply to hug her. She is a remarkable hero.

Even Larry King was touched, saying, "You know what you learn from this show? The determination of the human spirit. I mean, really, you can say it's freaky and all these kinds of things, but basically these are people doing what we couldn't do....With determination and skill and love. That's a great mother."

Finally, there is the highest form of sacrifice that comes from a genuine love and compassion for all beings. Mother Teresa was a hero who exemplified this stage by putting love into action. Every waking day, she selflessly gave of herself to care for the sick, the poor, the hungry, the dying, and the destitute. She embraced the people that society had abandoned with her compassion. Mother Teresa had a tremendous impact on the world through her moral example and inspired and challenged many leaders to follow in her path.

Interestingly, the original meaning of the word hero comes from the Greek root *servos* and *heros*, which means 'to serve and protect' (incidentally the motto of the Toronto Police). Self-sacrifice for the higher good and betterment of humanity is at the heart of being a Hero or Leader.

I want to forcefully point out here that the root definition of hero centering on self-sacrifice and service to others is incredibly important in our development. It implies that the seeds of greatness lie within us all, and that we can all endeavor to become the heroes we were truly meant to be. Martin Luther King Jr. really brought home this point when he declared, "Everyone can be great because anyone can serve. You don't have to have a college degree to serve. You don't even have to make your subject and your verb agree to serve...You only need a heart full of grace. A soul generated by love."

VISION

"Without a vision, the people will perish."
– Proverbs 29:18

Great heroes have great vision. They are 'larger than life' characters who dare to dream. They have a vivid vision in their minds that is astonishingly clear. Heroes are the producers and directors of their own lives who write their own scripts. Using their faculties of imagination, our heroes have the ability to see their future up close with all their senses and in much detail.

This incredible power of imagination is what Walt Disney called, *'imagineering.'* Disney dreamed up his theme park and the wonderful characters that would come magically to life to entertain generations of families years before their fruition. When others saw nothing and ridiculed him, he saw the future. Walt Disney was a hero who not only had hindsight, but also *mindsight.* The Oxford Dictionary defines hindsight as "wisdom about an event *after* it has occurred." Great minds, in comparison, have mindsight: wisdom about an event *before* it occurs.

Leonardo da Vinci was a man who had powerful mindsight. "Da Vinci wrote these prophetic words on his sketch of the first flying machine: 'Man shall grow wings.' His Machine did fly a few feet, but Church leaders of the day, labeling it an instrument of the devil, forced him to destroy it. Time proved da Vinci right. Now men and women truly do have wings!" [Taken from Dr. Robert Anthony's, *The Ultimate Secrets of Self-Confidence.*]

If the people of Leonardo's era were to be transported in a time machine to the present, I'm sure they would be frightened to behold the massive jetliners that cut so frequently through our skies today – mistaking them for terrifying, fire-breathing dragons. The people of his day were afraid of such mind-shattering, revolutionary thoughts because they were afraid of the unknown. But Leonardo da Vinci was not afraid. He was certain. So certain, that he could literally taste the future when he boldly proclaimed to the world: "When once you have tasted flight, you will forever walk the earth with your eyes turned skyward, for there you have been, and there you will always long to return."

In mythological fables of the hero journey these magical powers of foretelling the future are often referred to as sorcery. It is what led Einstein to declare, "Imagination is more powerful than knowledge." In more recent times, these 'prophetic' powers, are described as clairvoyance, and relegated to gypsies and the paranormal. This, of course, is all nonsense. There is nothing occult-like or paranormal in the least. We all have the power to imagine. But it requires work and concentration to dream. Most people don't have the energy, patience, or time to use these faculties. What the majority of people don't realize is that once these faculties are tuned and used more often, it becomes child's play. Just watch children. They are completely immersed in their own imaginary worlds. For children, imagination is fun and comes most naturally. A hero, too, retains his or her childlike wonder.

Ridley Scott, in his epic movie, *The Gladiator,* had a great vision to resurrect the glory of the Roman Empire and the gigantic majesty of the Coliseum. He imagined the grand panorama in his mind, in all its detail, even before it was recreated. He **saw** every detail, from the fighting gladiators in the pit, to the cheering, blood thirsty crowd, to the gods smiling down upon man's folly as the scorching sun set upon Rome. He **smelt** the stench of the coliseum floor drenched with the blood of a thousand unnamed heroes. He **felt** the terror of a gladiator before the fight. He **heard** the Olympian battle cry, of a fearless warrior among the trembling masses. He **tasted** the sweet wine of the gluttonous Emperor, Commodus, preparing to be entertained by death. And then, as all geniuses do, he went even one step further into the sixth sense: he **listened** to the symphony of his heart, as all these sensations and emotions stirred within, awakening the inspiration to recreate Rome in all its glory.

Millions upon millions of people around the world lined up to pay for this one little moment of truth. Why? Because this man had a great vision, and a team that believed in it. A hero finds a cause, a vision, that is greater than himself - larger than life; and in doing so, becomes 'larger than life.'

Muhammad Ali is a perfect example of just such a larger than life character. Here was a man with extraordinary vision. When he was a little boy, he looked up out of the family car and asked his mother, "Momma, what's that flashing sign called?"

"Oh, that's a marquee," his mother replied.

"Well, my name's gonna be on a lot of those marquees, Momma!" proclaimed Ali.

Here was a great man who declared to the world that he *was* 'Heavyweight Champion of the World.' He believed. He had faith: the ability to see the unseen. When everyone else thought he was either crazy or just making a lot of noise, Muhammad Ali *knew* he was 'The Greatest.' He more than just knew - he *was* the 'Heavyweight Champion of the Whole Wide World.' He was the Champ in his own mind and soul, before the people declared him so. He saw the triumphant glory of ultimate victory. When others just saw a cocky, black kid from Louisville, Kentucky, Ali saw the Olympic Gold medal draped around his neck - and beyond. Ali is the quintessential modern day hero: a fighting champion, a visionary, a leader, a role model, and a revolutionary. He is the ultimate hallmark of triumph over great struggle. He delivered to the world a little moment of truth. That is why Ali will be remembered forever as a true hero.

THE POWER OF FOCUS

"We succeed only as we identify in life, or in war, or in anything else, a single overriding objective, and make all other considerations bend to that one objective."
– Dwight D. Eisenhower

When researching the biography's of great people and interviewing very successful people, I got a strikingly consistent answer on how they became successful: "I had a dream, and stuck to it with focus and determination."

With laser-like focus, and unswerving concentration, they carried out their objective with the trenchant zeal of a crusader. Absolutely nothing got in their way. No obstacle was too big to surmount; they would go under, over, around, or break through any barrier that came their way. Every failure in life served as a stepping stone to the top of the mountain of success. And they would either be waving on top of the mountain, victorious, or lie dead at the bottom. It was all or nothing.

The attitude all these great people embodied was: come hell or high-water, it was 'California or Bust,' echoing the fiercely determined and enterprising spirit of the great pioneers, during the 1848 California Gold Rush of the wild, wild, West - in pursuit of the American Dream. And that is the winning attitude that the hero of today must embrace.

On Sunday, April 8, 2001, history was made at the Augusta National Golf Club as Tiger Woods won his second Masters and also became the first golfer ever to hold all four major titles at once. It was the greatest feat in modern golf history that left people in total awe and disbelief. People just could not believe how a man so young, could get so far, so fast. That day was a defining moment in sports history, making Tiger Woods a heroic icon for the epitome of victory. Then to top it all off, he went on to win his third Masters the following year, becoming the youngest player ever to own seven majors! And there seems to be no end in sight.

That kind of success doesn't 'just happen.' It's no secret that Tiger Woods spends the majority of his time preparing and training for the game: studying sports psychology, nutrition, and physiology, watching videos of his game performances, getting coached by the best, following a regimented physical training schedule including aerobics, stretching, and weight training, practicing with other golf greats on unfamiliar terrain, and continual refinement of his technique.

But why all this preparation? After all, it's just a game, right? Wrong! Not if you want to compete professionally. The only purpose for Tiger, and all winners, is to play the game – and win. Tiger publicly admitted this truth himself when he turned pro: he plays only to win. That's the focus. That's the discipline of a champion. Tiger said it best, "I focus only on what I can control – my game – despite conditions."

In his book, *How I Play Golf,* Tiger talks about how his Dad trained him, at a very early age, to focus the powers of his mental concentration to withstand any and all distractions. When teaching his son golf, Earl Woods established two basic rules. The first rule was no talking during a round. Earl did everything in his power to distract his son, from dropping a set of clubs in the middle of Tiger's backswing, to walking in his line of sight as he was stroking a putt.

The second rule Earl set was that there were no more rules. Anything could happen. Tiger's father had no idea how much strain his son could take, so they both agreed on a secret word (equivalent to saying, "mercy") that would be Tiger's out if he couldn't handle the pressure. Either out of stubbornness or sheer determination, Tiger never used the word!

All this training centering on mental toughness, discipline, and focus, paid off in the end, and helped Tiger to be well prepared for the real-life distractions of the game: competing players trying to throw him off with a cold hard stare, camera shutters going off in the middle of a swing, or the negative energy from a crowd. There are all sorts of distractions in life. How focused and determined are you to winning the game of life?

Taking the concept of focus to a larger scale, listen carefully to the enduring words of John F. Kennedy and pay close attention to the emotions they arouse in you:

"First, I believe that this nation should commit itself to achieving the goal, before this decade is out, of landing a man on the Moon and returning him safely to the Earth. No single space project in this period will be more impressive to mankind or more important for the long-range exploration of space...But in a very real sense, it will not be one man going to the Moon - if we make this judgment affirmatively, it will be an entire nation. For all of us must work to put him there...

This decision demands a major national commitment of scientific and technical manpower, material and facilities, and the possibility of their diversion from other important activities where they are already thinly spread. It means a degree of dedication, organization, and discipline which have not always characterized our research and development efforts. It means we cannot afford undue work stoppages, inflated costs of material or talent, wasteful interagency rivalries, or a high turnover of key personnel.

New objectives and new money cannot solve these problems. They could in fact, aggravate them further - unless every scientist, every engineer, every serviceman, every technician, contractor, and civil servant gives his personal pledge that this nation will move forward, with the full speed of freedom, in the exciting adventure of space."

President Kennedy's Special Message to the Congress on Urgent National Needs May 25, 1961 (Delivered in person before a joint session of Congress) John Fitzgerald Kennedy Library Columbia Point - Boston, Massachusetts 02125

Does this sound like the words of a madman? A Lunatic? A foolish daydreamer that builds castles in the air? Hardly. Here was a man who proclaimed to the world, with laser precision, the single-minded objective of sending man on the moon before the decade was out. And, by God, he did send man on the moon! On July 20th, 1969, before the decade was out, U.S. Astronaut Neil A. Armstrong, of Apollo 11, became the first human to step on the lunar surface, and made history by uttering his now famous words, "That's one small step for... man; one giant leap for mankind."

John F. Kennedy had a dream, a vision to send man on the moon and return him safely to Earth before the decade was out. When he made that prophetic statement, he said it with such force and conviction that his people believed him. His goal was specific, with a time limit. He rallied the full and undivided support of his entire nation, and every scientist, every engineer, every serviceman, every technician, every father, mother, and child dreamed with him – the miraculous adventure of space travel.

It was an exciting time that galvanized his country around one single objective that had to be achieved at all costs. It was as if all the elements of his nation, like a magnet, were all facing in one direction to **attract** the one goal, of the same kind.

What makes a magnet a magnet, with its power to attract, is simply when all its elements face in one direction. It is a scientific fact that everything in life is made out of these common elements. Even our own blood has a magnetic force field. And that is the universal power of focus. To make our dreams a reality, we need to focus all our elements, all of our resources, on the one primary objective at hand.

ACTION

"Action is eloquence." – William Shakespeare

I'm sure you've probably heard the saying, "There are three types of people in the world: those who watch things happen, those who wake up and ask, 'what happened?,' and those who make things happen." Heroes make things happen. They just do it. Doesn't matter whether they are feeling good or lousy, they do it. Heroes are very decisive. They are great thinkers, but they are even greater ACTors. They take massive action which generates massive results; hence the deserving cliché – 'Action Hero.' They get things done with little or no words.

When a reporter asked Pierre Trudeau how far he would go to fight terrorism, the Prime Minister of Canada replied defiantly, "Just watch me!" And that was it. That was all he needed to say. The rest was action, and the army was shortly called out to guard Parliament against terrorist attacks from the radical FLQ Quebec separatists. "Just watch me." It's the signature phrase of a true hero implying action speaks louder than words.

Action becomes the essence of the hero soul. It is an integral part of the hero's character. Heroes have such an intense vision, that they 'out picture' the rest by going out and doing what no one else is willing to do. It is said that love conquers all. Yet love is practiced through action. How we act and react in crisis shows how great, or lacking, our love really is. It is one thing to proclaim one's love for another. But to actually show one's love by doing, especially when the other person is struggling through some hardship, is quite another undertaking all together. Heroes practice love by doing.

People mistakenly think that great heroes are always fearless. That is not true. They are human after all. Heroes also have to cope with fears and inner demons. What sets the hero apart from the average person is that heroes act 'in spite of' fear. They face fear in the face, and do the thing they fear. Heroes echo the sentiments of Carl Jung: "If there is a fear of falling, the only safety consists in deliberately jumping."

Not only do heroes act in spite of fear, but they often take on the most difficult challenge first. While others are trembling and paralyzed by fear, not knowing which problem to tackle first, the hero often chooses to tackle the one they fear most. By doing so, they leap in full force. The forceful impact of the challenge is absorbed in their system. This gives them greater capacity to handle even more difficult challenges along their journey.

There is a great epidemic scourging our society called fear. Fear causes inaction, and ultimately shattered dreams. People are afraid to make mistakes in life because they are paralyzed by the fear of rejection. "What will people think of me if I fail?" That is the question that goes through their mind over and over again. Unfortunately, they attract what they focus on the most: failure! Even worse, their inaction throws them into a tailspin, entering into a vicious cycle of procrastination, repeated failures, and eventual sedation to the comforts of mediocrity.

Heroes break the common mold by defying convention. Convention says, "Ready, Aim, Fire." Heroes say, "Ready, Fire, Aim." Except in the rare cases of major, pivotal decisions that do require some careful thought before proceeding, heroes, for the most part, act first and ask questions later. They realize that too much analysis leads to paralysis. Instead, they keep taking action every day knowing that they can make the necessary corrections along the way. And in the end, they reap all the rewards.

STRENGTH

"...Those who hope in the Lord will renew their strength. They will soar on wings like eagles; they will run and not grow weary, they will walk and not be faint."
– Isaiah 40:31

The legendary heroes of myth all show great physical attributes of strength: enormous size, powerful muscles, the ability to leap over tall buildings, to bend steel, to crush the skull of an enemy with their bare hands, to literally carry the weight of the world on their shoulders, and on and on. Images of strongman Heracles, the classical hero of Greek mythology, more widely known by his Roman name, Hercules, are conjured up when one thinks of superhuman strength. Heracles, the son of Zeus, was known to be the strongest mortal, and even stronger than many of the gods.

So strong was Heracles, that he was summoned by the Olympian Gods themselves to help them fight and win their final battle against the Giants, after they defeated the Titans. Despite his physical strength, Heracles lacked intelligence and wisdom. Even worse, he had no control over his emotions and was very hot-headed. This got him into a lot of trouble as he was easily offended in his wounded pride.

What people often do not realize is that many of Heracles great feats of labor were done as a result of doing penance for foolish acts that he committed in his fits of rage or general carelessness. One of his first tasks was to clean up the Augean Stables in which for many decades cattle had dropped their dung. This was certainly not a fitting task that would be assigned to a hero of substance, character, and great inner strength.

We can learn from the ancient Greeks, by understanding that their heroic tales of great physical achievements are mythic and symbolic representations of strength. For true heroes have more than just physical strength, but also strength of character and condition of mind. Heroes need to be strong in mind, body, and spirit in order to successfully accomplish their mission.

Make no mistake, heroes do take care of themselves physically. They have a daily regimen that includes physical training, aerobic exercise, and healthy eating habits for peak levels of fitness. Physical fitness makes one sharp minded and ready to do battle. About the many benefits of exercise, Nelson Mandela wisely mentioned in his autobiography that, "Exercise dissipates tension, and tension is the enemy of serenity. I found that I worked better and thought more clearly when I was in good physical condition, and so training became one of the inflexible disciplines of my life."

Physical exercise helps one to think clearly, stay alert, and reduce anxiety and depression. More importantly, exercise improves self-esteem and boosts confidence. This is because by exercising we get the double benefit of feeling a natural high with the release of pleasure producing endorphins while also feeling good about ourselves. Exercising tells your soul that you care about your body and have respect for your self.

For the hero soul, always seeking higher and higher plateaus of expansion, physical exercise is only the beginning to developing a strong condition of mind. Condition of mind involves a sense of discipline and dedication to nourish and tune the mind, body, and spirit – to nurture all aspects of the total human being.

How does a hero develop a superior condition of mind?

Before heroes go into battle, they sharpen their sword, an extension of their body, and they sharpen their mind and spirit through meditation, prayer, and quiet reflection. They summon the gods above to give them strength and to help and guide them in their journey. They think and plan for success and condition their mind to win the battle even before it is fought. Sun Tzu, the great 6th century Chinese philosopher, exemplified this mindset of the victorious warrior more than two thousand years ago in his epic work, *Art of War*:

"When your strategy is deep and far-reaching, then what you gain by your calculations is much, so you can win before you even fight. When your strategic thinking is shallow and near-sighted, then what you gain by your calculations is little, so you lose before you do battle. Much strategy prevails over little strategy, so those with no strategy cannot but be defeated. Therefore it is said that victorious warriors win first and then go to war, while defeated warriors go to war first and then seek to win."

A victorious hero needs to spend enormous amounts of time preparing and conditioning their mind for success. A hero with the greatest condition of mind will always be able to defeat the physically stronger opponent who is of weak mind and fails to plan for victory. The hero's 'strength' is total and complete.

TRIUMPH OVER STRUGGLE

"Accept the challenges, so that you may feel the exhilaration of victory."
– George S. Patton

Surpassing struggle is a uniquely transformative experience. It gives the hero the capacity to handle greater and greater challenges. As a result, the hero enjoys far greater rewards than most people could ever imagine possible. By overcoming, heroes transcend their limiting life problems and transform themselves into pure gold. They are the real alchemists of our time - transforming lead into gold. Through the applied pressure of struggle and the knowledge to overcome, they transform their dark coal minds into precious diamond minds. And thus is born a superior way of living.

Some days life seems so tough and discouraging that one feels like throwing in the towel and giving up. Whether it's trying to get that next appointment with a potential client, trying to publish one's book, searching for one's soul mate, or looking for a meaningful career in a difficult job market, the ongoing challenges of life have the tendency to grind us into the ground. The ability to not only effectively cope with struggle but to be positively transformed by it, is the mark of a true hero. When others are ready to throw in their towels, the hero says, "I'm going to pick myself up, get back on my feet, and redouble my efforts. I *will* win! I *will* succeed despite the odds." They have the will to overcome. Heroes stand the test of time. Time and patience are the greatest allies of the hero soul.

People love working with heroes because they show them how to conquer their own fears. When they see heroes overcoming insurmountable odds and persevering over difficult times, they have a new found respect for them and want to do business with them, to be associated with them, and to follow them. The hero has *earned* their respect. Respect has to be earned. It is not something that just happens. The living message that the hero projects to humanity is: "through facing and conquering life's challenges we are transformed."

Struggle allows us to grow and cut through superficial ego - to go deeper into truth. We become better human beings with rare depth of understanding, wisdom, and grace. It is nature's way of allowing beauty to unfold within us. Quitting early only defeats us, limiting our lives to the ugliness that we have created.

What do I mean by this? Just observe nature. When a caterpillar is in its cocoon, it begins struggling with great effort to get out. If you were to 'help' the caterpillar out of its naturally occurring maturation process, it would turn ugly, rot, and die. Nature has a purpose and design for everything. The caterpillar's struggle is necessary so that the vital life force in its body flows into its budding wings. As the caterpillar vigorously expends effort in its cocoon, the vital, sustaining life juices flow into its wings. The caterpillar is thus transformed into a beautiful butterfly.

The hero transcends struggle to achieve victory. He or she triumphs over great adversity, and in so doing, inspires the world. The hero ultimately has the wisdom and capacity to react positively in the face of hardships. That is what separates the ordinary from the extraordinary. Depth of character is proven by how one chooses to react in difficult times. For those who choose to live in doom and gloom, believing life is a struggle, I have news for you: life is *not* a struggle! Struggle is only a small part of life. It must be swallowed and overcome or it will swallow you.

To the hero, pain is inevitable, while misery is optional. Heroes understand that nature plays its course whether we like it or not. It does not take sides. Its power is experienced by all. There will be pain in life. But it is how we choose to react to tragedy and pain, which makes a difference. We can choose to see the good in every situation or we can see nothing but misery. We can learn from our failures and move on, or allow failures to defeat us. The choice is ours to make.

Great heroes go beyond just reacting to pain. They challenge themselves, *before* life challenges them. They prepare the way a world champion boxer prepares for the great fight: taking as many blows or failures from life to absorb the pain in their system. These trials and tribulations strengthen the hero heart and allow the hero greater capacity to overcome what Shakespeare called 'the slings and arrows of misfortune.'

The ogres and demon monsters that guard the doors between time and eternity, between the known and unknown, take great pains to ensure the hero is thoroughly tested before they allow him or her to pass. But once the passage is made, the hero is initiated into the circle of herohood. When you reach that stage, doors will open that you never knew existed and your dreams will manifest instantly. You will finally be treated with the respect and recognition you deserve and you will be honored as a world citizen.

The Rock and Roll Legend, Tina Turner, exemplifies this type of hero who triumphs over great struggle. In her moving autobiography, *I, Tina*, she documents her trials and tribulations and her rocky, whirlwind of a marriage to singer, Ike. Ike was an unfaithful and terribly abusive husband who flew into such violent fits of rage that he frequently beat Tina with phones, shoes, hangers, and anything he could find.

One day, while his wife was touring with him, Ike punched Tina's face so hard that her jaw broke. Yet, somehow, she managed to find the strength to sing to a large crowd that very same day – the fresh blood still gushing in her throat.

It was times like this that Tina found it so difficult to cope. One day she even tried taking her own life by swallowing all fifty sleeping pills in a little bottle of Valium. It is a miracle beyond my comprehension that she survived that experience! With no money, four children to look after, and a raging, abusive man for a husband, where did she find the strength to go on? The answer: through her faith in God.

Tina Turner personally found strength in her Buddhist faith. The first acknowledgement in her autobiography goes to the spiritual teachings of a 13th century sage named Nichiren Daishonin whose teachings are practiced by a world-wide Buddhist organization called Soka Gakkai International, of which she is a member. It is well documented in Tina Turner's autobiographical movie, *What's Love Got To Do With It*, how she converted to Buddhism and started chanting 'Nam-myoho-renge-kyo' (Hail to the wonderful Lotus Sutra!) over and over again to draw inner spiritual strength.

But it really doesn't matter what spiritual orientation you are. If you have faith in the Higher Power that created you, you will be able to overcome even the most trying of times. Tina Turner herself acknowledged this truth by admitting, "The real power behind whatever success I have now was something I found within myself – something that's in all of us, I think, a little piece of God just waiting to be discovered."

On the **Larry King Live** show, aired February 21, 1997, Larry King paid tribute to Tina Turner by saying, "You are a heroine. You are a citizen of the world. Any place you hang your hat is home. This has been a delight. Thank you."

I love this hero for her courage and inner strength to overcome. She is forever young. Tina Turner gives us all hope to believe in our dreams. She is 'simply the best.'

MASTERY

"We are what we repeatedly do. Excellence, then, is not an act, but a habit."
– Aristotle

Heroes are in love with excellence. They are Warriors of Excellence. Heroes go above and beyond action: they achieve mastery in their work by practicing the fundamentals to perfection. In their pursuit of excellence, their consistent actions turn into habits, which become their character. They are the best of the best, because they give their absolute best. And just when they think they've given the best they could possibly give, they strive to go beyond. They are professionals.

The samurai, Japan's ancient warrior class, were true professionals in their own right. They were highly skilled in fighting and the use of psychological warfare. They had unparalleled skill in swordsmanship, the martial arts, use of the bow and arrow, and were able horsemen. Not only did they achieve mastery in the art of fighting, but also achieved mastery of mind. They disciplined and controlled their mind by following the Bushido Code, or Way of the Warrior, based on honor, justice, bravery, and loyalty. Because of this, they were respected and feared throughout the land.

To be respected and feared in 9th century Japan, a country that held honor above all else, was a sign of greatness and remarkable accomplishment. The samurai were the best of the best. To acquire the status of samurai, literally meaning 'to serve,' did not come easily, nor was it taken lightly. It required years and years of practice, mental discipline, and mastery of the fundamentals. The samurai would practice fencing until the blade became an extension of themselves. One swift blow could kill their enemy in the blink of an eye.

Mastery was a lifelong way or commitment for the samurai. They practiced the fundamentals of martial arts over, and over, and over again, for years, until it became a part of them; until they could react in their sleep, without thinking, and expect the unexpected. With mastery the samurai is able to perceive the unknown, and penetrate the depths of his enemy's soul. With mastery the samurai does not think, but acts. For thinking is deadly. A moment's thought is the kiss of death. A samurai does not think, but acts. He acts from being, not doing.

Many people forget they are human beings and become human doings. They are blinded by their day to day busyness and become like sheep: following the rest of the herd – to be slaughtered by mediocrity. They are fooled into thinking that because they are doing lots in their busyness that they are getting somewhere. In reality, they are just running around in circles exhausting themselves. Action must spring from a strong sense of purpose that comes from having a high degree of self-knowledge, knowing exactly what one wants in life, and how one will serve others along the way.

Today's samurai, or Warriors of Excellence, act from being. They act from a deep sense of knowing who they are by tuning with their soul. Character is developed only from the mastery of purposeful actions that become habits. Our habits shape our character. And our character ultimately determines our destiny.

The legendary actor and filmmaker, Sidney Poitier, is a Warrior of Excellence. Serving more than fifty years in his profession and appearing in over 40 films, Mr. Poitier is a role model who will be remembered for spinning movie magic: delivering moments of truth to the world.

Mr. Poitier once said, "I think the way I want to think. I live the way I want to live." That is the mark of a man who knows who he is and operates from a deep sense of conviction. He exemplifies a man of mastery, dignity, poise, and grace.

Born in such extreme poverty that his mother had to make his pants from flour sacks, to now being on Walt Disney's Board of Directors and serving as Ambassador to Japan for the Bahamas, Mr. Poitier has certainly come a long way.

In 2002, Frank Pierson, the President of the Academy of Motion Picture Arts and Sciences, presented Sidney Poitier with an Honorary Oscar for his "extraordinary performances and unique presence on the screen." As Mr. Poitier began his acceptance speech, a hushed silence of awe and deep reverence fell across the entire auditorium. Upon finishing his speech, the entire audience gave him a standing ovation. That day he lifted the spirits of millions of people around the world. People were moved and deeply touched to the bone for the years of excellence he had portrayed on and off screen that came about from the skillful mastery of his craft.

After the awards ceremony, Mr. Poitier was asked if there had "ever been a time in a film where he felt in complete control of his craft." He emphatically replied, "No." For Mr. Poitier, there was "always room for improvement, always room for change, always room for betterment."

Even though, at 75 years of age, he had just won an Honorary Oscar for a lifetime of achievement, Mr. Poitier had the humility to acknowledge that true mastery comes from the never-ending pursuit of excellence.

In 1967, more than three decades before receiving this Honorary Oscar, Mr. Poitier was given an even greater honor by Dr. Martin Luther King, Jr. who said, "He is a man of great depth, a man of great social concern, a man who is dedicated to human rights and freedom. Here is a man who, in the words we so often hear now, is a soul brother." [Taken from THE JOHN F. KENNEDY CENTER FOR THE PERFORMING ARTS.]

Sidney Poitier is billed as the first African-American to have won the Best Actor Academy Award in 1963 for *Lilies of the Field*. He defied the odds and made his mark. He defied the Hollywood of his time and paved the way for generations of young African-Americans to follow in his footsteps. But Mr. Poitier goes well beyond being an African-American treasure. He is more than an American treasure. He is a treasure to the world - a Prince of Light! His example of mastery through the constant pursuit of excellence will shine the world over.

SILENCE

"The rest is silence." – **William Shakespeare,** *Hamlet*

Silence is the great source of inspiration. When our minds are empty, out of the still, dark silence, new ideas give birth, and our souls are renewed. The hero speaks the language of the gods from the place where dreams are born. They speak to the gods in silence. They listen in silence. The hero's code of silence is magnetic. Hypnotic. It draws people to them, like the ocean. People are soothed by their calm oasis and become charged in their presence.

Heroes speak only when they have something to say. Their words carry weight and significance, and people stop and listen to what they have to say. Heroes realize they have one mouth and two eyes and two ears for a good reason, and they exercise that: spending most of their time observing, sensing, and listening.

Unfortunately, most people speak far more often then they listen. They are too busy talking about trivial affairs, gossip, and wasting valuable energy. Instead, they could be planning their lives and taking action towards their dreams. Sad to say, but most people 'pass gas' from both ends of their bodies. Heroes do not waste time. Time is their most precious commodity.

Silence has a lot more to do than just conserving energy. Practicing silence through still reflection or meditation is about clearing the mind and emptying the cup. If the cup is always full, one cannot receive.

You don't always have to sit still like a statue and meditate all day to benefit from silence. It could be a walk in the park or forest. You can practice the art of silence through painting, sailing, swimming, yoga, horseback riding, canoeing, hiking, mountain climbing, skiing, camping, sculpting, carving, sewing, or just lying on the grass, like a kid, and watching the clouds go by. You might even be tempted to build a sand castle by the beach. Well, go ahead, nobody is stopping you. Be like a kid again!

When you relax and keep quiet, the genius is heard. A great well of spontaneous creative power springs up from the non-thinking silence. For silence is the language of the gods. They whisper sweet tales of the hero journey. Instantly, you are transported to a parallel universe; a magical land where your double is already living your dreams and experiencing the deepest desires of your heart.

That is why children are so creative. Have you ever seen a child play? When a child 'make believes' he is Peter Pan flying over the Tower of London, how could you possibly argue that he isn't really Peter Pan? He *is* Peter Pan!!! For the child has momentarily entered the parallel universe and taken the place of his double.

Be like a child. The Bible exemplifies this message in Matthew 18:1-5:

"At that time the disciples came to Jesus and asked, 'Who is the greatest in the kingdom of heaven?' He called a little child and had him stand among them. And he said: 'I tell you the truth, unless you change and become like little children, you will never enter the kingdom of heaven. Therefore, whoever humbles himself like this child is the greatest in the kingdom of heaven...'"

Silence, like nature, is that great humbling force. Practicing the art of silence in our daily lives puts us in tune with the great Sun Child within – the hero soul.

THE SHADOW: Seven Deadly Sins

"A violently active, intrepid, brutal youth - that is what I am after... I will have no intellectual training. Knowledge is ruin for my young men."
– Adolf Hitler

Real modern day heroes, compared with mythic heroes, have their faults. Heroes have a larger than life attitude involving great ambitions and fierce determination. This leads to very intense, fiery emotions. Emotions, if gone unchecked, that can cause massive destruction and evil if steered in the wrong direction. It is what George Lucas in *Star Wars* refers to as the 'Dark Side of the Force.' It is our shadow side. Lucifer, the once light-bearing throne angel of God who fell from grace, is the shadow of Divinity. Divinity is within everyone, but so is the devil. If heroes do not prepare for and understand their shadow side, they run the risk of becoming absolute monsters.

Before we explore the dark side, please note that these two chapters respectively titled *The Shadow* and *The Angel* are separated only for the purpose of delineating the villain and the hero in their *perfect* states. This is done so we can clearly see the two opposites of the same coin that lie within us for our own psychological growth and understanding the dramatic function of each for character development. The reality is that no one is perfect and both villain and hero reside within us all. In order to experience true greatness both have to be integrated into our lives for a holistic approach that expands our awareness of who we are and what we are capable of. Subsequent chapters will show us how to tap into this powerful creative force that is limitless.

In psychology, the term 'shadow' was coined by Carl G. Jung to represent the hidden, nefarious impulses of our personality that we see as undesirable and have tried to repress. The shadow is not the whole of the unconscious, but contains all the undesirable aspects of ourselves that we hide from society behind our social mask or persona. Taken to the extreme, some people go too far by repressing and denying their negative impulses to win the approval of others. This form of self-deception is dangerous because these repressed, dark impulses eventually surface to wreak havoc with unforeseen actions and consequences.

It is important to realize that the shadow does have some good qualities such as normal instincts and creative impulses as well as undeveloped emotions and desires that can become positive if we consciously learn to use them. We will explore this aspect of confronting the shadow and harnessing its power for good in the chapter titled *Tuning With The Hero Soul*.

For our purposes of understanding the dark side, in this chapter we will only explore the shadow aspect of the pure villain. The psychology of the villain consists primarily of the seven deadly sins: arrogance, envy, laziness, greed, hatred, lust, and gluttony. The fusion of all 7 destructive emotions results in the villain-demon or pure monster. Because heroes are passionate in everything they do, they run the risk of being overpowered and blinded by these strong emotions that lie within us all, causing damage not only to themselves but others around them. In extreme cases they can become enormously destructive such as with Hitler, Mussolini, Lenin, Marquis De Sade, David Berkowitz (Son of Sam), Charles Manson, Al Capone, Jim Jones, Pol Pot. Movies have portrayed these characters more dramatically as Darth Vader, Hannibal Lector, Scarface, Colonel Kurtz (Brando in *Apocalypse*

Now), Norman Bates (*Psycho*), Max Cady (De Niro in *Cape Fear*), Tommy DeVito (Joe Pesci in *Goodfellas*), and the *Sexy Beast* (Ben Kingsley).

Many heroes end up in some form of leadership role tenaciously supporting a cause for the people. Ironically, this steely determination can often turn into the vilest form of greed where winning at all costs with no regard for others becomes the chief aim. CEOs, generals, and political leaders are especially susceptible to these afflictions. Their shadow weaknesses are pride, ruthlessness, greed, and vanity. They can become so ferocious and ruthless in their pursuit of success that their people become paralyzed through fear. Their arrogance and self-glorification causes them to ignore all criticism because they feel they are above everyone. Their greed causes them to sometimes be unfair in their dealings, becoming bullies. Eventually, their emotions betray them, turning on themselves. The negative emotions turn into a black, hideous, toxic waste literally poisoning their bodies and turning them into villains.

In the villain's all consuming greed, he or she wants more power, more money, more pleasure, and more acquisitions. It's never enough. The villain is always coveting and never satisfied. They are always comparing to see who has more and want what they have. That is envy. Villains feel resentful for another person's advantages and have a strong desire to possess them. Carrying envy to the extreme, they want to literally possess and replace that person at all costs – including murder. The villain, in his twisted state of mind, believes he can get away with murder by projecting his own inner evil onto the person he wishes to posses. The evil act of murder then becomes justifiable in his eyes and the reprehensible sin is committed.

Let's explore some of the other destructive emotions that embody the shadow side. Because heroes can be so passionate, sensual, and intensely experiential in everything they do, they can often fall prey to lust and its close cousin, gluttony. These two powerful emotional forces have destroyed many lives and ruined the ascending careers of many heroic figures. Experiencing deep cravings for the often elusive feeling of that ultimate high, the peak sensation of pleasure, heroes (as with all of us) can often lose their patience and control, and yield to temporary pleasures that can destroy them.

Some heroes who lose control of their emotions tend to go all out and burnout – fast – like a shooting star. In their greed to reach the top in the shortest amount of time, they often take short cuts, and cheat themselves with momentary pleasures that can become addictive, such as lustful sex, gambling, drug and alcohol abuse, excessive smoking, or overeating. In the process, they can lose their health, their self-esteem, their high standing, their families, and their careers. Too many examples of heroes giving in to destructive shadow forces abound: Elvis Presley, Janis Joplin, James Beluchi, Magic Johnson, Marilyn Monroe, Jimmy Hendrix, Gary Hart, Jimmy Baker, Jim Morrison, Richard Pryor, Ernest Hemingway, Howard Hughes. Instead of judging, we can all learn from their mistakes.

When sex becomes an object of desire, without love and without respect for the other, both victims can end up wanting more and more only for their own immediate pleasure. They often can't get enough and it becomes an addiction. People usually use drugs for the same reason; they have lost self-respect and self-love, and desire momentary pleasure to fill the emptiness and cut the pain. But pretty soon, the addiction begins to consume their thoughts and their lives. When and how they can get their next 'fix' becomes forefront in the mind.

This loss of respect for self and others causes people in turn to disrespect them with equal measure. It becomes a vicious cycle. Self-esteem further deteriorates. Because they have no self-respect, they often can become gluttonous, recklessly feasting and partying without care. Eventually they lose interest and discipline in their work, becoming lazy and careless. Their empire begins to crumble before their very eyes and all that they've worked so hard for begins to slip away.

By losing all self-respect, the hero begins to hate himself and others. He can become envious and spiteful towards others. Hate is one of the most destructive emotions. Hate stems from fear. Fear of the unknown. Fear comes from ignorance - a lack of knowledge on the laws of how the mind works and how the universe operates. Fear is caused due to a lack of knowledge about one's self, about one's soul, about their true potential, about humanity and the workings of the world around them. All fear originates from the state of not knowing.

When a warrior goes into battle unprepared, not knowing anything about the capabilities of the enemy, not knowing his own capabilities, and not even knowing that he does not know, he becomes afraid. Because he instinctively does not want to show his fear, the fear turns to anger. He becomes angry because he is confused and does not know what to do, for he lacks knowledge. His anger turns to hatred. And hatred causes him to react with blind fury towards the enemy. He lashes out haphazardly like a fool, and in his folly of rage, is easily destroyed by the enemy. Because the warrior had no strategy, no plan, no knowledge, he became an easy prey for the enemy to entice him into anger and foolish actions.

Hatred can be turned inwards, inflicting harm and damage on one's self, or it can be turned outwards towards other people. The outcome remains the same – tragic destruction. Once a hero succumbs to hatred, he has given himself over to the 'Dark Side of the Force.' When all the negative emotions are carried to their extreme, he becomes a pure villain: a horrific, unfeeling monster. The psychology of the villain embodies all the destructive emotions.

One of the best ways to check these emotions is by practicing the seven virtues, or opposite emotions of the seven deadly sins. The highest form of hero is the Angel. Angels are the perfect fusion of the seven virtues, which will be covered in the next chapter. Here is a summary of the dual opposites:

PSYCHOLOGY OF THE HERO SOUL

The Hero - Angel	The Villain – Demon
Seven Virtues	**Seven Deadly Sins**
1. Humility (humbleness)	1. Arrogance
2. Contentment	2. Envy
3. Industry	3. Laziness
4. Generosity	4. Greed
5. Love (patience, serenity) *	5. Hatred (anger)
6. Chastity (being in love, eroticism)	6. Lust (addiction)
7. Moderation	7. Gluttony

* Please note: I do not consider love to be the 'dual opposite' of hate. This is just for illustrative purposes to show that by practicing patience and serenity we can begin to love. While hate is the fusion of all negative emotions, love is the fusion of all the positive emotions, and more: it actually swallows, consumes, and contains all the negative emotions as well. Love is wisdom. Love is God. Love encompasses all.

THE ANGEL: Seven Virtues

"Lost in awe at the beauty around me, I must have slipped into a state of heightened awareness...Self was utterly lost. I and the chimpanzees, the earth and trees and air, seemed to merge, to become one with the spirit power of life itself."
– Jane Goodall

The penultimate hero is the complete opposite of the villain. Where the villain embodies the seven deadly sins, the hero practices the seven virtues: humility, contentment, industry, generosity, love, chastity, and moderation. The Angel is a perfect fusion of these positive, light-emanating emotions. These emotions are mirror opposites of the seven deadly sins.

Angels are pure light, the closest beings to Divinity, and the highest path a hero can ascribe to. Gandhi, the Dalai Lama, Buddha, Jesus, Muhammad, Mother Teresa, Nelson Mandela, Confucius, Martin Luther King Jr., Daisaku Ikeda, John Lennon, Joan of Arc. These are some of the great and venerable souls that come to mind when I allude to the higher stages of herohood.

In this elevated plane of being, heroes have the power to manifest their dreams and realize their vision. They can perform miracles. They have the power to inspire the people of the world. They are prepared to break on through to the other side where Divinity dwells and are skilled in bringing back the boons of the netherworld back to their people. From the spinning of pure light, they are able to create and recreate new worlds beyond anyone's imagination. By practicing the seven virtues, we can at least begin the ascending path of higher realization and actualization of our most cherished dreams.

Let's look at humility, the state of being humble. It is the first virtue and mirror opposite of arrogance. Humility is one of the most powerful virtues of all, and also the most difficult to practice, because it involves annihilation of the ego. Ego gets in the way of people's good judgment, causing them to boast and to take offense easily. Ego causes wars, violence, and fighting to erupt because each party is too focused on proving their own limited view point as the 'right and just way.' The Ego is about ME!ME!ME! The hero soul is about WE. The Three Musketeers are a symbolic representation of the hero soul: "All for one, and one for all." Similarly, the Holy Trinity conveys the same message: the Father, the Son, and the Holy Ghost are One.

Humility is not just the sole domain of the hero saints such as Gandhi or the Dalai Lama. In fact, many top business leaders are humble. Henry Ford, Ray Kroc, Mary Kay, Lee Iacocca, Rockefeller, Benjamin Franklin, Walt Disney, Warren Buffet, Bill Gates, Dale Carnegie, all have exhibited varying degrees of humility. What made these people great was their ability to serve their customers and employees first and foremost. They didn't need to flaunt their power. What really drove them was the chance to continually service their customers. They were always looking to better the lives of people in some way. None of them stopped their mission when they amassed huge fortunes. They didn't say, "Okay, great. I've got all the wealth, all the toys, all the material possessions, I could possibly need. I'm just going to go on a permanent vacation." No. They chose to serve and continue serving.

Jesus exemplified servant-hood by healing the sick, restoring sight to the blind, making the crippled whole, guiding and teaching his people, feeding his people, and ultimately giving his life on the cross for humanity. To be truly great is to be humble, to put aside one's ego and serve people.

Jesus spoke frankly to his disciples on this topic, and it is an important leadership lesson to remember: "...Whoever wants to become great among you must be your servant, and whoever wants to be first must be slave of all. For even the Son of Man did not come to be served, but to serve, and to give his life as a ransom for many." Mark 10:43-45.

After humility comes contentment, the opposite of envy. It's a sincere feeling of fulfillment and gratefulness. The hero soul always focuses on the good in life and is full of gratitude. Heroes are perpetual optimists even in times of struggle. They enjoy the journey just as much as looking forward to reaching their destination. They happily achieve instead of trying to achieve happiness. Heroes are too busy serving other people and being thankful for the blessings in their life to waste their energies being envious of others.

Industry, the opposite of laziness, comes from doing what one loves and deriving a sense of satisfaction and meaning from one's work. The reason why superheroes are able to accomplish far more than anyone could possibly imagine is because they have an extraordinary vision that is much larger than themselves. Having such an enormous vision gives them an endless supply of energy and industry. Industry is more than action. It is *massive* action on a large scale to meet a desired end.

Heroes are also very generous souls; they are generous with their time, their money, their teaching, and their work. Where greed destroys, generosity creates. The more generous you are, the more the universe will bless your life, creating even more wealth, health, and happiness. To paraphrase from Proverbs 11:24, "Life gives to the giver and takes from the taker." Again, it comes back to service. Heroes feel it's their duty to give. Muhammad Ali said it best, "Service to others is the rent you pay for your room here on earth."

While villains give in to anger, heroes practice patience and serenity. Patience comes from the Latin root 'pax – cienga' or the 'science of peace.' Heroes study the science of peace. They are serene and tranquil like water. Where the villain is easily angered, heroes are as calm and poised as can be. They practice the art of patience and serenity every day. They listen to nature and tune with the rhythm of nature. Heroes take time to meditate everyday withdrawing into the silence of eternity. By practicing patience and serenity one can begin to love.

Chastity, the opposite of lust, is a sense of purity and innocence. It is a childlike wonder and awe similar to falling in love for the first time. Although chastity is an emotional state of mind involving purity of thought and self-control, which helps reduce negative addictions, it is also erotic in nature, harnessing the power of eros. Eroticism is an exaltation of sexuality where lust can be a degradation of sexuality. Eroticism honors sexuality as a beautiful and divine experience. It is like two lovers admiring each other's naked bodies and walking hand in hand without any shame, guilt, or feelings of dirtiness. Wouldn't it be great if we could fall in love all over again with our partner? If we could fall in love with life with every rising and setting of the sun? What an exhilarating and empowering emotion that would be!

Moderation, the opposite of gluttony, is what separates the pros from the amateurs. Amateurs are impatient and want to get everything done right away. They sprint to what they think is the finish line, only to realize that they haven't even reached the starting point, and tend to burn out quickly. Although life does call for moments of sprinting, heroes are generally marathon runners, slowly chipping away at their goals every day, in a very disciplined and often easy-like manner. An amateur thinks they can do a 100 push ups and be fit for life. A hero knows that the key to healthy living is eating a moderate portion of meals, and having a simple and moderate daily exercise regimen.

Finally, love is the greatest and most creative and inspiring emotion of them all. It is also a difficult concept to understand let alone explain. Telling someone to practice love does not really accomplish much without understanding the true nature of love. First of all, love is not the 'dual opposite' of hate as many people are led to believe. While hate is the fusion of all negative emotions, love is the fusion of all the positive emotions, and more: it actually swallows, consumes, and contains all the negative emotions as well. Love is wisdom. Love is God. Love encompasses all.

For our practical understanding, love is the *awareness* of all these emotions, good and bad, combined with consciously *acting* on this knowledge to do good. For how can we love without showing empathy and compassion for others that can only come from realizing our own shortcomings and saying, "But there for the grace of God go I"? And what is the use of knowing the definition of love without practicing it?

The foundation of love is respect. By practicing patience and serenity, the hero empties and quiets the mind. From the emptiness and silence, inspiration emerges and begins to rise into conscious awareness. Inspiration is divine knowledge inhaled. It is knowledge of one's soul, knowledge of the mysteries of the universe, and knowledge of the truth that Divinity dwells within every human being. From this higher awareness, springs respect and compassion for others. For one cannot help but to give and to respect people when they see God in every being. Respect, then, is the foundation of love.

Jesus, Prince of Peace, gave the world a truly noble definition of love in Corinthians 13: 1-13:

"And now I will show you the most excellent way. If I speak in the tongues of men and of angels, but have not love, I am only a resounding gong or a clanging cymbal. If I have the gift of prophecy and can fathom all mysteries and all knowledge, and if I have a faith that can move mountains but have not love, I am nothing. If I give all I possess to the poor and surrender my body to the flames, but have not love, I gain nothing.

Love is patient, love is kind. It does not envy, it does not boast, it is not proud. It is not rude, it is not self-seeking, it is not easily angered, it keeps no record of wrongs. Love does not delight in evil but rejoices with the truth. It always protects, always trusts, always hopes, always perseveres. Love never fails...And now these three remain: faith, hope, and love. But the greatest of these is love."

TUNING WITH THE HERO SOUL

"That I feed the hungry,
forgive an insult, and love my enemy –
these are great virtues.
But what if I should discover
that the poorest of the beggars
and the most impudent of offenders
are all within me,
and that I stand in need
of the alms of my own kindness;
that I myself am the enemy
who must be loved –
what then?"

– C.G. Jung

Unless you're looking to become a monk or saint or want to risk having a personality split resulting in neurosis, trying too hard to be perfect by blindly pursuing the light, while ignoring the darkness, can be disappointing. You can never *become* perfect, because you already *are* perfect. Although as fallible human beings, we do have flaws that we call imperfections that need to be recognized and corrected, real perfection or truth, lies at the core of our being. And truth contains both good and evil. Trying to become perfect, trying to be who you're not, is moving away from the source of perfection that is already within you.

The truth is that good and evil cannot exist without the other. Light has no meaning without darkness. For darkness gives birth to the rising sun. In the darkness of night one can view the canopy of brilliant stars above shinning brightly like an ocean of sparkling gems. It is darkness that gives light its radiant beauty. Love is not good. Nor is it bad. Love is wise. It contains both good and bad. Love is the truth. And the truth shall set you free.

There are still too many people today, especially in the personal development camp, who seem to be singing the same 1940's song, "You got to latch on to the affirmative, eliminate the negative, accentuate the positive, and don't mess with Mr. In-between." I think it's time to change that tune.

It's not about positive or negative thinking. If it were that easy we would all be healthy, wealthy, and wise through positive affirmations alone. Many people today sense that something vital is missing from their lives and still do not know their purpose or passion in life. The reality still remains that most people on earth are just barely coping with their day to day lives – the vast potential inside them left untapped.

It's not about positive or negative thinking. Positive and negative thinking *both* stem from our belief systems. Our beliefs come from our level of awareness. To achieve greatness, we must first change our current level of awareness. We need to expand awareness of ourselves, of our true potential, and of the world around us. Having a high degree of self knowledge and self acceptance prepares you to tune with the hero soul.

The soul is our bridge between the human machine and God. The soul is defined as the awareness of our thoughts, emotions, desires, and will. By expanding your awareness, you expand your soul. This is the great hero quest that many are trying to achieve. It is what Carl Jung meant when he said, "A sense of a wider meaning to one's existence is what raises a man beyond mere getting and spending. If he lacks this sense, he is lost and miserable."

Within us are many competing, converging, and changing energies. We must achieve higher awareness and integration among these often contradictory forces, to achieve balance, wholeness, and healing. This process of integration: seeking self-knowledge, self-acceptance, and wholeness is what Carl Jung referred to as individuation. It is the ultimate Grail Quest and spiritual journey in which we become truly ourselves. By consciously taking this hero journey, you will eventually reach that magical moment when you can take off your mask, look within, and find your true calling – your purpose in life and the work you were meant to do. This will bring you much joy and inner peace.

Confronting and learning from your shadow, or dark side, is one of the most important first steps in this mission. While ignorance leads people of the world to fight holy wars amongst themselves, heroes fight the holy war *inside*: confronting and annihilating their own demons. His Holiness the Dalai Lama said, "The enemy is our guru." This enemy can also be the enemy within. The well-rounded Renaissance Hero not only explores the light, but also the darkness – the qualities of the villain within.

Shakespeare, who was not only a great poet, but also a true Renaissance Hero and leading thinker of his day, understood this concept clearly even before the birth of psychology as we know it. In his rousing war epic, *Henry V*, Shakespeare eloquently writes:

"Gloucester, 'tis true we are in great danger;
the greater therefore should our courage be.
Good Morrow, brother Bedford. God Almighty!
There is some soul of goodness in things evil,
would men observingly distil it out;
for our bad neighbour makes us early stirrers,
which is both healthful and good husbandry.
Besides, they are our outward consciences
and preachers to us all, admonishing

that we should dress us fairly for our end.
Thus may we gather honey from the weed,
and make a moral of the devil himself."

– Henry V: **King 4:1:1-12**

Referring to the enemy as our 'outward consciences,' Shakespeare touched on a profound concept in psychology called projection. Projection is a destructive form of self-deception where we refuse to see our own worst faults, and instead, see these same faults in others. Through projection, we hide our own dark motives and 'project' them onto others.

The supervisor who publicly criticizes her employees for being lazy, selfish, and late for work, and yet always arrives late, delegates her own responsibilities to subordinates, and takes frequent and lengthy breaks at the company's expense, is a real life example of projection that happens all too often in the workplace. The results of such self-deception include: alienation, stagnant growth, loss of respect and ill-will from coworkers, and ultimately the loss of one's ability to effectively perform their job duties resulting in termination.

Projection can also happen collectively with the masses such as when the Nazis deluded themselves into thinking they were cleansing the Aryan race of 'impurities.' Hitler was a delusional madman who subconsciously described his own worst faults by projecting his evil nature onto Winston Churchill when he declared:

"For over five years this man has been chasing around Europe like a madman in search of something he could set on fire. Unfortunately he again and again finds hirelings who open the gates of their country to this international incendiary." [Hitler's description of Churchill. Taken from Carl Jung's book, *Man and His Symbols*]

To break free from this self-deception, we need to confess our sins. By confronting our own shadow and admitting our faults, we learn to exorcise our own demons. The leaders that admit their imperfections and take full responsibility for their failures are easier to like than those who do not. By having the courage to risk rejection and be yourself, you become a hero.

How does one practically assimilate the shadow into one's waking consciousness and turn undeveloped emotions of the dark side into positive energy? The answer does not have to be difficult: it starts from awareness. Paying close attention to the negative emotions that are stirring within you, realizing the consequences of these emotions, and consciously deciding to change, can sometimes be enough to bring about transformation.

To find answers we need to ask questions. By asking yourself powerful questions such as, "Why am I experiencing this negative emotion?", "What is the deeper cause of this emotion?", "What is trying to happen?", "What will be the consequences if I yield to this emotion swelling inside me?", and "How can I turn this negative energy into positive energy?", you raise your level of awareness and tune with your soul so you can begin to take control of your destiny.

Many people, for example, at some point in their lives feel an onset of depression and the resulting fatigue that further stifles their ability to enjoy life. There are many factors that can cause depression. A very common cause, if one were to really examine *why* they were experiencing this depression, is resistance to change. Fearing change, people get caught in a rut of daily routine and sameness which can totally destroy creativity. Eating the same food, hanging out with the same friends, doing the same work, shopping in the same neighborhood, and carrying on the same day-to-day routine can bring on a feeling of hopelessness and depression because the possibilities and opportunities in life seem limited. But the reality is that the possibilities are only limited by one's lifestyle.

If these people were to look closely at the consequences of continued depression (stagnation, boredom, dullness, stress, fatigue, physical ailments, neurosis, insanity), there would be sufficient motivation to take action. They would realize that what's trying to happen is change. From this awareness they could convert depression into an exhilarating feeling of adventure by doing something different: eating out in new, exotic restaurants, taking a painting or dancing or creative writing course, changing their wardrobe, changing their furniture, going away on a road-trip or long train ride, listening to new music, meeting new friends, joining new clubs. Doing just about anything different would break the monotony and change their lives for the better! The hero is the champion of things becoming – always changing with the times.

So many problems and unnecessary violence in the world can be avoided just by raising our level of awareness and exploring the consequences of unchecked emotions of the dark side. It is really sad to see the daily tragedies unfold before us in the drama of life because of this lack of awareness.

A compelling example of unchecked negative emotions gone astray can be seen in the January 25, 2002 Cambridge, Massachusetts' rink-rage case of 'hockey dad,' Thomas Junta, who was sentenced six to ten years for the fatal beating of his son's hockey coach, Michael Costin. It started off innocently enough when Mr. Junta saw another player elbow his son in the face during a noncontact hockey scrimmage being supervised by Mr. Costin. Junta, understandably angry, yelled at Costin to stop the rough play, and Costin in his own fit of anger snapped back, "That's hockey!" The two men then got into a scuffle that was broken up.

But Junta, in his rage, came back at Costin, and witnesses testified that Junta, the 44-year-old, 6-foot-1, 270 pound truck driver, pinned 156 pound Costin to the floor and repeatedly struck him in the head. In the wake of his towering rage, Mr. Junta left the four children of Mr. Costin fatherless, his own wife and two children with a convicted father in prison, and a lifetime memory of another man's spilt blood that will haunt him forever.

The positive aspect of anger is energy. Anger, as a shadow emotion, can be transformed into energy that can be channeled into doing something positive and productive about the situation that caused our anger. But the shadow cannot be transformed unless we first know that it exists. What really struck me in the rink-rage case was the sheer amount of brute force applied by Mr. Junta. Junta assaulted Costin with such extreme force that he almost decapitated the hockey coach. That act required a lot of force - a tremendous amount of energy. Energy that could have been channeled into industry to build another ice rink and a new junior hockey league dedicated to hockey as a clean sport.

By understanding *both* the psychology of the hero and the psychology of the villain that lie within us, we begin to understand our true nature. Only then can we assimilate the shadow into our waking experience by transforming our dark, hidden motives and undeveloped emotions into a wider vision. As a villain, greed will consume everything in your path – including yourself. As a hero, your all consuming greed can be transformed into the life of a connoisseur with an appreciation for the finer things in life, instead of the wretched life of a glutton.

In the end, you must clearly choose your path. Choose to be a villain or a hero, but do not waiver, like a coward, in between. For as the Great Teacher taught, be thou cold or be thou hot, but do not be lukewarm or life will vomit you! For those of you that have made it this far into the book and have chosen the path of herohood – I salute you. Your journey will be a most rewarding one.

ACCESSING THE UNKNOWN

"The difference between what the most and the least learned people know is inexpressibly trivial in relation to that which is unknown."
– Albert Einstein

Ronald Reagan paid tribute to the astronauts that perished in the Challenger space shuttle explosion of 1986 by concluding in his stirring speech, "The crew of the space shuttle Challenger honored us by the manner in which they lived their lives. We will never forget them, nor the last time we saw them, this morning, as they prepared for their journey and waved goodbye and 'slipped the surly bonds of Earth to touch the face of God.'" I am convinced that the Challenger crew would have experienced the same fate had they survived and the space shuttle continued on its course.

Had the Challenger crew penetrated the new frontier of space and looked out their spaceship's porthole to behold this majestic round earth with its swirling mass of clouds, like a tiny, blue marble hanging silently in the dark vastness of space, they would have been instantly transformed. As Dan Millman pointed out in his book, *The Laws of Spirit*, they would have, like so many astronauts before them, left the earth as scientists and returned as spiritual beings with a new heightened awareness of the Spirit.

The Spirit will never die, because the Spirit was never born. It was, is, and always will be. Experiencing the Spirit, the unknown, awakens and illuminates the hero soul within. It led Einstein to declare, "The most beautiful experience we can have is the mysterious. It is the fundamental emotion that stands at the cradle of true art and true science. Whoever does not know it and can no longer wonder, no longer marvel, is as good as dead, and his eyes are dimmed."

Tuning with the soul through self-knowledge and self-acceptance is not enough in itself to achieve the greatness we long for. To reach our purpose in life and to effortlessly achieve the deepest desires of our heart, the unknown has to be accessed and its deep spiritual powers activated, releasing a flood of healing and creative energy that transforms us and moves us to do greater things than we ever thought possible.

How do we tap into the unknown to accomplish this? This chapter will be devoted to covering this question. Here are seven key methods, which we will discuss further, to accessing the powers of the unknown:

ACCESSING THE UNKNOWN

1. **Going Beyond the Limit**
2. **Dreams & Creative Imagination**
3. **New Experiences**
4. **Religion & The Arts**
5. **Meditation**
6. **Prayer**
7. **Archetypes**

The whole concept of breaking on through to the other side and penetrating the unknown may at first glance seem quite daunting and mystical. It doesn't have to be. I want to de-mystify this process so people can realize that *anyone* can achieve greatness through the right application of higher knowledge. In other words, you don't have to be highly intellectual and you don't need a PhD to experience a passion for greatness. Let us now explore the seven ways of accessing the hidden powers of the unknown:

Going Beyond the Limit

Anytime you push yourself to go beyond your perceived limits, you enter the zone of the unknown. If you normally can only do 60 pushups to the point of total exhaustion but one day summon all the strength and willpower you have to surpass that arbitrary limit by doing another 20 pushups, you have entered the realm of the unknown. This is that magical moment when you don't quite know how you did it, or what's possible, or what's going to happen next. In this moment you have experienced the mysterious – where anything is possible.

All this requires is a leap of faith; a sense of certainty that there is a Power that is greater than you and which has no limits. And then, you take the plunge. If you've never sat in total silence by yourself (without any distractions such as the TV, radio, or thinking about your future) for more than 20 minutes, deciding to one day experience silence for 40 minutes is a leap into the unknown.

If you're used to spending an hour on weeknights working on a project such as writing a book but leave the weekends for partying, you could choose to devote 12 hours on weekends for the first two months. If you're in sales and you've never booked more than 10 appointments on any given week, you could decide for one week, and only one week, to book 15 appointments whatever it takes. Even if that means waking up earlier to devote one extra hour of cold-calling every day to break your supposed 'threshold' to accomplish your objective. Remember, it's only for one week. After that you can go back to your old ways. But I guarantee you will never be the same. Once you've crossed your threshold, you activate the powers of the unknown to enter into your waking consciousness. You initiate a new learning experience that cannot be undone. By going beyond the limit, your awareness expands along with the possibilities open to you.

Dreams and Creative Imagination

The dreams of the whispering wind enter my heart
and permeate my soul
to tell of a tale untold
yet fully known and once traversed
bringing me back to the place I cry for
in all my wandering days on earth.

These were my own first words which spontaneously sprung from my unconscious to share with you the significant impact I feel dreams have in one's quest for deeper meaning.

Dr. Vivianne Crowley mentions in her book, *Jung: a journey of transformation*, about how Carl Jung broke away from Freud's main school of thought to redefine modern psychology: "Jung believed it was a search for meaning, not a satisfaction of sexuality [as Freud proposed], that was the most powerful motivating force for humans...He perceived that in all times and places humankind had engaged in the spiritual quest. This was the most powerful human urge of all – to be at one with the Divine Self within."

Along the same vein, Jung broke new ground by suggesting that the unconscious was not a mere depository of past remnants but a wellspring of inspiration with new creative ideas, visions, and prophecies that never existed before. In his own words, Jung felt that "what we consciously fail to see is frequently perceived by our unconscious, which can pass the information on through dream...Dream symbols are the essential message carriers from the instinctive to the rational parts of the human mind, and their interpretation enriches the poverty of consciousness so that it learns to understand again the forgotten language of instincts. [Taken from Jung's *Man And His Symbols*.]

Jung believed that dreams, being a specific expression of the unconscious with meaning, are both causal and purposive and should be treated as fact. By treating your dreams as 'fact' and consciously exploring the meaning behind the language of your dreams, you activate the powers of the unknown to guide you, warn you, heal you, solve problems for you, and to generate a flow of rich ideas that will inspire you to new heights of achievement, creativity, and innovation.

Time and time again, history has shown that conscious awareness, reverence, and understanding of one's dreams have led to immense cultural enlightenment and scientific advancement. Kekule, the 19th-century German chemist, discovered the molecular structure of benzene through a dream in which he had a vision of a snake swallowing its tail (an ancient archetypal symbol). He interpreted the dream to mean that the structure was a closed carbon ring. Thus the Benzene Ring became a concept which revolutionized organic chemistry.

Einstein dreamt of riding on a beam of light and noticed that space-time became curved which helped him formulate his world-paradigm shattering theory of relativity. Walt Disney dreamed about many of his now famous cartoon characters including Mickey Mouse. Charles Dickens got the inspiration for many of his memorable characters through his dream notes. Some of Thomas Edison's best inventions came to him in his dreams. Mary Shelley's tale of Dr. Frankenstein was originally inspired from her own tormented dream that soon followed after the death of her newborn daughter. Mary Shelley wrote of her unspeakable grief in her journal: "Dreamt that my little baby came to life again . . . that it had only been cold, and that we rubbed it before the fire, and it lived. Awake and find no baby. I think about the little thing all day. Not in good spirits." [Marry Shelly, *Journal, 19ᵗʰ of March, 1815*]

Descending from the mountains, the Prophet Muhammad gave to his people the Koran (Reading), the sacred scripture of Islam with all 114 of its chapters called *suras*, which came to him as revelations of God through a dream. After days and nights of prayer and meditation, Prophet Muhammad fell asleep in the cave of Hira and was visited by Archangel Gabriel in a dream. Gabriel appeared before the frightened Muhammad and commanded the forty-year-old, illiterate man to recite passages that were dictated from Allah (God). With a power unknown to him, Prophet Muhammad began to recite the passages that would serve as the pillar of light-emanating spiritual wisdom – elevating an entire civilization.

When recounting these revelations that Prophet Muhammad received, many religious scholars cautiously shy away from using the word 'dream' and prefer to use the word 'vision' instead, because they think dreams are commonplace occurrences that are not from God, whereas 'visions' come directly from God. I believe that nothing could be further from the truth. Dreams and visions can be used interchangeably and *both* come from God.

Prophet Muhammad himself spoke of the origin of dreams: "Now Allah has created the dream not only as a means of guidance and instruction, I refer to the true dream, but He has made it as a window on the world of the unseen." And in Job 33:15, the Bible clearly mentions, "For God does speak – now one way, now another – though man may not perceive it. In a dream, in a vision of the night, when deep sleep falls on men..."

The important thing to remember is to not dismiss your dreams as just trivial mishmash of the day's events but as factual information that is alive and intelligent with a purpose. You must treat your dreams with reverence and love if you wish to benefit from them as all the legendary greats did before you. Keep a dream journal by your bedside to record your dreams. By taking some time to read up on dream symbolism and interpretation (Carl Jung is a good source to start from) your life will be greatly enriched with meaning and new power.

I strongly encourage you to make an effort to understand and enter into dialogue with your dreams. If something is disturbing you in your dreams you can use what Jung called 'active imagination.' Through active imagination you imagine the dream scene again, as best as you can remember, and confront what's troubling you. Perhaps you've been having a recurring dream of being chased by a monster. You can re-imagine the same dream sequence in meditation and confront the monster and ask it what the matter is or how you can help. Or you could consciously decide, before going to sleep, that if you have a similar dream you will become conscious of the dream and confront what's haunting you. This is called a *lucid dream* where you become aware of the dream as it is occurring and begin reshaping the outcome as planned the night before.

All these methods are a function of creative imagination, where you are creatively using your God-given tool of imagination to create or co-create your future. The ultimate act of creative imagination is when you can imagine how you want to see yourself in the future with such conviction and clarity that your mind will accept it as fact. This is the moment when you experience heaven on earth, when you begin living your dreams now!

New Experiences

It will be a momentous day when this book reaches the generation whose average citizens can economically travel into space. Most of us however might not have the opportunity, in our lifetime, to travel into outer space to experience a higher perspective that transforms our soul. This does not preclude us from searching for new experiences that will expand our awareness.

Anytime we undergo a significantly new experience in our lives we tap into the unknown. When you take the leap of faith and endeavor to experience something never tried before, you enter the realm of the mysterious; not quite knowing what to expect you activate the powers of the unknown.

Traveling to foreign countries is the best way of accomplishing this. However, if you travel without making any effort in getting to know the culture and instead cocoon yourself by practicing your own familiar customs, eating your own traditional foods, and surrounding yourself with friends from your own country, you will gain little benefit and might as well stay home.

Enjoying new experiences requires insatiable curiosity and marvel. Expand your horizons by really experiencing a new culture: visit their historical landmarks, befriend the locals to experience a shared humanity, try on new clothes and new customs, listen to their music, sing their songs, dance to a new tune, visit their temples of worship, taste the exotic flavors your tongue is not accustomed to, and pay attention to how they conduct commerce and solve problems differently from your own. By doing this you will enjoy a wealth of knowledge that will empower you. Experiencing the unknown will open up your soul and expand your awareness of what is possible.

Religion & The Arts

Both religion and the arts draw from each other. Art experienced at the highest level can become a profound religious experience, and likewise, a peak religious experience can become a deeply poetic moment of supreme beauty.

By reading classic literature such as Hemingway, Tolstoy, Goethe, Schopenhauer, Emerson, Thoreau, Mark Twain, Charles Dickens, Nathaniel Hawthorne, Rumi, Kahlil Gibran, Shakespeare, Nietzsche, Victor Hugo, and the Greek myths, you enrich your mind and begin to penetrate the mysterious. In his autobiography, Nelson Mandela writes about how uplifting he found reading the classics: "I had read some of the classic Greek plays in prison, and found them enormously elevating. What I took out of them was that character was measured by facing up to difficult situations and that a hero was a man who would not break even under the most trying circumstances."

A similar experience can be taken from viewing a classic painting or sculpture done by Michelangelo, Da Vinci, Van Gogh, Monet, Rodin, Picasso, Rembrandt, Dali, etc. By looking into these marvelous masterpieces you penetrate the soul of genius. Classical music can also be enormously uplifting and inspiring. Mozart, Beethoven,

Bach, Handel, Brahms, Chopin, all composed symphonies that were nothing less than Divine.

There is nothing wrong with experiencing contemporary works. After all, the classics at one time were 'contemporary.' I find for example watching a really good movie or reading a compelling story from a new author can have just as much of a powerful, moving, and transformative experience. But the classics have always stood the test of time.

Religion provides a window into the unknown. Learned scholars, prophets, and seers have all spent years if not their entire lifetimes exploring the mysteries of the unknown and documenting their wealth of wisdom in ancient sacred texts such as the Vedas, the Koran, the Torah, the Bible, the Tibetan and Egyptian Book of the Dead, and the Tao te Ching. By taking the time to read some of this profound spiritual wisdom, you stand on the shoulders of giants. I also encourage studies in understanding world religions such as Islam, Christianity, Buddhism, Judaism, and Hinduism.

Immersing yourself in this knowledge will lift your heart and elevate your level of perception to a higher plane. As you read and understand, realizing that the Divinity dwells in all, you will become less and less fearful of the world and feel a rising confidence surge within you. By becoming aware of the common humanity that cuts through all race, class, creed, and color, you will never be intimidated by anyone regardless of their rank, status, or social position. And if anyone ever looks down on you, even if they are at the highest executive or political level, you can meet their cold stare with an equally unyielding look of steel that says, "You cannot intimidate me. Nobody is better than me. Nobody is above me or below me. I am entitled to the same greatness and glory under the rising sun!"

Meditation

Many highly successful people from different cultural backgrounds and different parts of the world have found meditation to be enormously beneficial to their success. Meditation calms the mind and soothes the soul. It provides a means to clear your mind of troubling thoughts so you can focus on what is important. Meditation is ultimately an effective communication medium between the known and the unknown, where the Divine speaks and you listen.

Meditation is just a way in which you clear your mind to listen to what God has to say. It makes you more receptive to intuition, ideas, and inspiration. There are many different meditation techniques but they all share something in common: simplicity. Don't be fooled by charlatans who try to convince you of how complex the art of meditation is so they can justify charging large sums of money. The simpler and easier it is to practice the better.

The art of meditation involves the following: a sincere willingness to quiet the mind, deep breathing from the diaphragm, paying attention to the flow of breath going in and out of you, relaxing the muscles and mentally letting go, being still and silent so you can listen to your inner voice, and you may also choose to include a visualization of what you desire, an affirmation of what you want, a consciousness lifting chant or mantra (Om), or just concentrate on an object such as the center of a rose thus clearing your mind of any distractions to reach a higher state.

There are thousands of good books on how to practice meditation. Pick one that suits you best and begin practicing. Some of the 'side-effects' you will enjoy include a healthier immune system, less stress, a peaceful serenity, mental alertness, a reduction in the workload of your heart, your level of intelligence and capacity to learn will increase dramatically, better physical coordination and improved athletic performance, enhanced job performance, increased ability to concentrate and focus, and in the process you will enjoy higher self-esteem. Wow! That's a lot of benefits for the peripheral side-effects of meditation. Fulfilling the main purpose of meditation is even more powerful.

The main purpose of meditation is to establish a direct connection with the unknown, with the Divine in you. When you plug into the source of creative intelligence by quieting the mind and listening in silence, you unleash the powers of the unknown to guide you. You will be given directions in fulfilling the promises in you. You will naturally feel impelled and compelled to act: to make that phone call, to begin writing, to join a club, to meet someone. Whatever the urge is, trust it and yield to it. It is the guiding light that will make your dreams a reality.

Prayer

Prayer is the opposite of meditation. Where meditation is a form of *listening*, prayer is direct communication with the unknown by *talking* to God or the Creative Genius. It is a form of communion where one lifts oneself from the earthly realm into the unknown and becomes transformed. For prayer to work one requires faith in a Higher Power. It is actually a natural extension of our soul for in times of great distress we all turn to God. By returning to this source for help, and not waiting for hard as a prerequisite, we draw forth power that is beyond anything we could possibly imagine or contain.

The best form of prayer is sincere, simple, and from the heart, with an attitude of gratitude. It requires effort on our part to do the things we can to change while having faith that our prayers will be answered. We also need forbearance to understand that the answer might not always be what we expected but that it will always serve as a gift to guide us along our path.

Prayer can be spoken out loud, thought in silence, or it can even be a feeling or longing with no words. It doesn't matter how you pray as long as it comes from the heart. The Bible recounts the story of Hannah, a wife who could not bear children, who visit's the priest, Eli, to pray at the Lord's temple:

"As she kept on praying to the Lord, Eli observed her mouth. Hannah was praying in her heart, and her lips were moving but her voice was not heard. Eli thought she was drunk and said to her, 'How long will you keep on getting drunk? Get rid of your wine.'

'Not so, my lord,' Hannah replied, 'I am a woman who is deeply troubled. I have not been drinking wine or beer; I was pouring out my soul to the Lord...'"   Samuel 1: 12-15

Her prayer was answered and she bore a son, Samuel, who became leader of Israel, and later she conceived five more children. Through faith all things impossible are made possible. Speak from your heart and pour out your soul in prayer. Be thankful for what you do have and you will be blessed with more. Pray for yourself, but also pray for others. This will help to eliminate the ego that limits your potential for greatness. Ask for strength and guidance. Ask for wisdom above all things. Wisdom will give you the discernment to use your abilities to achieve what it is you truly desire. And when you are stuck and don't know what else to do – ask for help.

Archetypes

Dr. Carl Jung believed archetypes are universal symbols and recurring themes that cause inner transformation and shape the myths of all cultures. These repeating psychic energy patterns or emotionally and spiritually charged images appear universally throughout human history, across all civilizations, and geographic regions. According to Jung, archetypes, like dreams, spring from the collective unconscious of the human race. The collective unconscious is a storehouse of inherited instincts and accumulated human wisdom shared by all. I believe it is a part of the World Soul or Gaia which consists of the unconscious instincts and psychic remnants of the entire human race as well as the combined consciousness or awareness of all existing humanity. It is but an eye blink, a momentary gaze upon eternity, the Divine.

By understanding these universal recurring themes, images, symbols, and characters that frequently appear in your dreams and the world around you, you will benefit greatly from the forces of the unknown that are unleashed within you. You will reach higher and higher realms of perception, creativity, and achievement. As you assimilate these archetypal energy patterns into your waking experience and realize that they are but many facets of your own personality, you will experience a transformative healing process that makes you a more complete human being.

We will now explore the seven central archetypes which have a powerful effect on us all. From these main archetypes a combination of hundreds of other archetypes are commonly derived. This chapter breaks down each archetype with answers to three questions: 1. What is its psychological function? 2. What is its dramatic function for creative purposes? and 3. What is its practical function? (I have taken the main format and structure of these seven key archetypes from Christopher Vogler's *The Writer's Journey* with some additional comments of my own.) The following are the seven archetypes:

THE SEVEN CENTRAL ARCHETYPES

1. **Hero**
2. **Mentor**
3. **Threshold Guardian**
4. **Herald**
5. **Shapeshifter**
6. **Trickster**
7. **Shadow**

HERO

This entire book can be considered a comprehensive study of the hero archetype. The hero embodies the journey from ego to non-ego; central to the hero theme is the dying of ego by humbling oneself and surrendering to a greater power in service to others.

Psychological function:
The archetype of hero represents the ego's search for deeper meaning and wholeness. It is the yearning for reconnection with the Divine. All the villains, demons, tricksters, mentors, lovers, guides, and seducers can be found within ourselves as aspects of our own personalities. We must penetrate the illusion that all these elements are separate and incorporate them all to become One.

Dramatic function:
The dramatic goal is to deliver an unforgettable moment of truth where the audience completely identifies with the hero. They see the hero's journey through her eyes. They experience the same enthusiasms, devotions, victories, heartbreaks, and defeats. The audience feels as if they have encountered growth with the hero. They feel as if they have experienced both life and death.

Practical function:
The only way to tune with the hero soul is to study it. Know the traits that make up the hero and the villain. Above all increase your awareness through self knowledge. Larry King, in his book *Powerful Prayers*, asked sports hero, Kareem Abdul-Jabbar, "For readers who may be interested in connecting to God, what advice would you give them?"

Kareem replied, "I would tell them to know themselves. You can't know anything beyond yourself until you know yourself. Where you begin and end – that's the whole concept. You have to understand that."

MENTOR

We are all familiar with the mentor archetype that commonly appears in our dreams, stories, and myth, often as a positive force that guides, initiates, supports, and trains the hero. This Force is the Divine acting through the universal character known as mentor which often takes the form of a 'wise old man' or 'wise old woman,' according to mythologist Joseph Campbell.

Many popular myths and stories have recognizable mentor figures such as Obi Wan Kanobi training the young Jedi Knight, Luke Skywalker, in *Star Wars,* Merlin the Magician guiding King Arthur, Glinda the Good Witch of the North helping Dorothy, or that crusty, cantankerous boxing coach in *Rocky* who barks at the Itallian Stallion, "You're gonna eat lightning and you're gonna crap thunder! You're gonna become a very dangerous person!" Although, sometimes the mentor archetype can also appear as the forever youthful 'eternal boy' or Sun Child of magical birth such as Cupid, Peter Pan, or Saint-Exupery's *The Little Prince* who declares: "Voici mon secret. Il est très simple: on ne voit bien qu'avec le coeur. L'essentiel est invisible pour les yeux. (And now here is my secret, a very simple secret: it is only with the heart that one can see rightly; what is essential is invisible to the eye.)" These child figures symbolize rebirth and renewal and serve as pure guiding expressions of the Divine, transforming darkness into light.

Psychological function:
Mentors represent the higher Self or God-within of the human psyche. This is the Force which penetrates all. It is higher, nobler, and wiser, and acts as our guiding conscience or symbolic parent. The mentor aspect of our personality exemplifies the highest aspirations of the hero.

Dramatic function:
In mythmaking, storytelling, and movies, mentors act as the great initiator into a higher realm of existence by teaching, training, coaching, and motivating the hero to carry out their mission. Mentors can also aid the hero's journey by giving a special gift that will become useful along the way. Examples of such gift bearing are prevalent in the arts: Obi Wan giving his protégé the light-saber, J.R.R.Tolkien's Gandalf giving Frodo the One Ring, the Good Witch of the North giving Dorothy magical ruby slippers, or "Q" giving James Bond the latest gadget which often becomes a lifesaver.

Practical function:
Actively seek out a mentor or a coach. Find someone who is very successful in life, preferably one who has mastered the profession or craft you wish to pursue whether it's in business, sales, acting, writing, sports, or any other endeavor. You can take the informal approach by befriending a role model or formally ask if he or she would be willing to be your mentor. Spend time with the masters; learn from them, model their behavior, get under their skin and find out how they think, what books they read, what their philosophy in life is. Ask them *how* they became so successful.

To achieve greatness you must give the best of the best of the best you can – and beyond. How is this possible? How can one possibly go *beyond* one's best? With the help and guidance of a mentor, you can accomplish this feat. Through their years of experience and wisdom, mentors will have a wider vision of what you can really accomplish and what's possible. Good mentors will enlighten you. Just when you think you've given your best, they will push and challenge you to achieve more.

THRESHOLD GUARDIAN

We are all on the hero's journey in the sense that we all encounter obstacles that need to be overcome on our adventure. Before the hero can penetrate the dark side to face and exorcise her demons, she usually has to overcome a menacing Threshold Guardian whose job is to thoroughly test her and see if she is ready to move to a higher realm. There is a powerful guardian at every threshold or gateway that leads to a new world or higher level of awareness. If one is not prepared to enter in mind, body, and spirit, access is denied.

Psychological function:

From a psychological point of view, these guardians stand for our inner demons: vices, repressed desires, emotional scars, negative emotions, low esteem, and the neuroses that limit our growth.

Dramatic function:

The main dramatic function of the Threshold Guardian is to thoroughly test and challenge heroes along the way. Usually the hero has to correctly answer a mysterious riddle, solve a puzzle, pass a test, or prove their strength to the guardian who blocks their entrance. There are many ways for heroes to overcome these obstacles: they can attack or kill their opponent, use trickery or deceit, become the guardian's ally, use bribery, intimidate the opponent, or momentarily become the enemy. In the movie, *Face Off*, an interesting twist happens when the hero, FBI agent Sean Archer (John Travolta), through radical surgery, 'borrows' the face of the villain, Castor Troy (Nicolas Cage) to penetrate the criminal underworld. Castor Troy in turn revives from his coma, faceless, and transforms into hero Sean Archer by surgically fusing the FBI agent's removed face onto his own. They both *literally* have gotten into each other's skin!

Practical function:

Don't be put off by outward appearances. Threshold Guardian figures, whether in your dreams or in real life, can appear to be intimidating. Whenever you reach a breaking point or *threshold* that will take you to a higher level, a threshold guardian will usually appear to frighten you away. They are really testing you to see if you have the guts and competence to move up.

Whatever you do, don't back off! Expect the challenge and be prepared for it. This happens in real life all the time: you want to meet with the CEO of a Fortune 500 company but the Executive Assistant keeps you at bay, you want to move up in the ranks and get promoted but the supervisor tries to break you down and keep you in your place, and even some of your 'friends' will do everything in their power to resist you and bring you back to *their* comfort level if you try to change.

But absolutely nothing can stop you if you are prepared and determined to move up. Be creative. Do your research. Get under the skin of the threshold guardian: find out what they like and dislike, how they operate, how they think, what their philosophy is, who they associate with, what their strengths and weaknesses are, and what motivates them. Move when they move. Sleep when they sleep. Momentarily become them, in order to transcend them. Through understanding you gain empathy. Through empathy the guardian becomes your closest ally.

HERALD

Often in the early stages of the hero's journey, a new force appears that challenges the hero and provides the impetus and motivation for significant change. This energy known as the herald archetype can be an event, an idea, a person, or a dream figure that forces the hero to make a decision that must be made. Up until this time the hero is getting by with the imbalance in their life and merely coping with day to day affairs. But when the decision has been made to follow the herald's 'call to adventure' the hero is transformed and nothing will ever be the same.

Psychological function:
The Herald figure plays the vital role of bringing to conscious awareness the need for change and appears in our lives when we are ready to undergo this change. It

could be an inner voice, a book we read, an accident, or a mysterious stranger that crosses our path. A chord is struck deep within the soul and change becomes inevitable.

George Lucas's success in the film industry came after a near fatal car accident in his senior year of high school that cancelled his plans to become a professional race car driver. Because Mr. Lucas was pronounced dead on the scene, he rightly felt he was given a 'new life.' He had to re-evaluate his life purpose and why he was put on earth. From that day onwards, he began living moment by moment on purpose. His life changed forever. The world is a better place because of George Lucas's passion and excellence in filmmaking.

Dramatic function:
Heralds get the story going and provide motivation for the hero to change. They alert the protagonist in the story as well as the audience that an adventure is about to begin or radical change is on its way.

A good example of the herald archetype in movies is the character of a juror, played by Henry Fonda, who is unconvinced of a boy's guilt who is accused of murdering his father in Sidney Lumet's masterpiece *12 Angry Men.* He stands up to the rest of the eleven jurors and challenges their unquestioning belief of the boy's guilt and their desire to end the trial quickly. In the First Act, Henry Fonda pulls out a switchblade he purchased from a local pawn shop and stabs it into the table. The blade is exactly identical to the supposedly 'unique' knife with special engravings used in the killing. The jurors erupt with heated arguments and the adventure begins.

Heralds can sometimes play emissaries of evil or villains whose role is to challenge and lure the hero into the dark side. In *Training Day*, Oscar winning actor, Denzel Washington, plays a corrupt cop who tries to lure a rookie police officer (Ethan Hawk), who wants desperately to join LAPD's elite undercover narcotics unit, into a dark criminal underworld. Denzel's character challenges the reluctant rookie to smoke confiscated pot laced with PCP and succeeds. "To protect the sheep," he tells him, "you got to catch a wolf. It takes a wolf to catch a wolf." Later he taunts the rookie by challenging him, "Are you a wolf?" Ethan's character responds by finally smoking the crack pipe loaded with PCP. Denzel in this case plays both herald and dark mentor to the uninitiated rookie cop.

Practical function:
Be aware of the herald archetypes or agents of change that enter your life and do not delay too long (except in the case of negative herald figures) in responding to their call for adventure. It is life's way of saying that it is now time to change.

The student in class might be a herald figure that publicly challenges the economics professor who lectures about successfully operating a business but has never ran a business himself. Maybe the professor has had a life-long dream of owning his own business. This is his wake up call.

Maybe that annoying salesperson that keeps 'following up' with you every month about that public speaking course is a change agent that is telling you to put aside your fear of public speaking and begin sharing with people your wealth of knowledge in the form of speaking. It could even be your friend who rudely points out the bulge in your belly and says it's time for you to lose weight. You may be offended, but as Churchill once said, "The truth is incontrovertible, malice may attack it, ignorance may deride it, but in the end; there it is." It's your wake up call for change.

SHAPESHIFTER

It can be difficult to understand the universal archetype of the shapeshifter because of its ever changing nature – always morphing and transforming its character traits. It is similar to the elusive energy found in water, electricity, or light. Light can sometimes appear as particles, sometimes as waves. The moment you examine its nature closely it changes appearance. The shapeshifter archetype is often encountered through the opposite sex, whose central characteristic is of a changing nature with unclear motivations, always keeping the hero guessing and introducing the element of surprise.

The shapeshifter, like water, is a symbol for transformation that represents the urge to adapt and change to ones environment for survival and procreation. It represents the universal impulse seeking the unity of opposites within us. Bruce Lee understood the power of this mystery when he said, "Be formless, shapeless. When you pour water in a cup, it becomes the cup. When you pour water in the teapot, it becomes the teapot. Be like water man!"

Psychological function:

The psychological purpose of the shapeshifter is to express the energy of the animus and anima, the male and female elements of the unconscious, to restore balance. We live in a society that still represses our opposite sex characteristics that lie within us. Not being able to express our true nature often leads to a host of neuroses and associated physical ailments.

The anima is the inner feminine aspect of the male psyche that is primarily shaped by a man's mother and his relationships with other women. The anima is essentially the female hero archetype that appears often in our dreams and acts as a mediator or priestess between the underworld of the unconscious and the mysteries of the spirit realm whose function is to bring knowledge from both realms into consciousness. Carl Jung believed there are four stages of development in the anima:

1. Eve is representative of the first stage which is biological, primitive, instinctive, and sexual.
2. Aphrodite, the Greek goddess of love, or Cleopatra represents the second stage and personifies a more feeling, romantic level.
3. The third stage is represented by the Virgin Mary, a figure who transforms personal love into spiritual devotion that gives rise to intuition.
4. Transcending figures such as Sophia (called Wisdom in the Bible), Sapientia (the Holy Ghost or Wise Old Woman), Mother Teresa, Shakti (the Goddess, the Power in the Heart), the Queen of Sheba, or the Mona Lisa painted by Leonardo Da Vinci, represent the fourth stage which is divine wisdom.

The animus is the inner masculine aspect of the female psyche which is shaped primarily by a woman's father and her relationships with other men. The animus is the male hero archetype that appears in our dreams as a mediator between the spirit realm and the underworld bringing truth into consciousness. According to Jung, there are also four similar stages of development in the animus:

1. Tarzan is representative of the first stage of wholly physical man symbolizing the animal, sexual realm.
2. Stage two can represent either the Knightly Lover, portrayed by romantic hero figures such as Sir Lancelot and Shakespeare's Romeo, or the Action Hero, typically portrayed by James Bond and Hemingway.

3. The third stage is the epitome of law, thinking, and high achievement represented by heroes such as Winston Churchill, King Arthur, and Henry V.

4. The highest evolution of the animus appears in the fourth stage as the 'wise old man,' seer, spiritual sage, shaman, saint, magician, or prophet. This is the most evolved state of the hero who becomes *The Messenger*, a carrier of truth. Gandhi, Merlin the Magician, the Dalai Lama, Jesus, Buddha, and the Prophet Muhammad are representative of this stage.

Dramatic function:
The shapeshifter introduces the element of surprise and brings doubt and suspense in the story. Many of the Hitchcock thrillers portray elusive, shapeshifting men whose motivations are unclear and keep the heroine doubting: "Can I trust him? Will he betray me? Does he really love me? Is he telling the truth? Is he being faithful to me?"

The *femme fatale* is a common dark-anima, shapeshifter archetype which introduces woman as a seductress or demon of death. Linda Fiorentino, in *The Last Seduction*, portrays a cool, calculating, sexually uninhibited woman who turns men into unsuspecting victims. Other examples of *femme fatales* include: Kim Basinger in *L.A. Confidential,* Sharon Stone in *Basic Instinct*, and Ellen Barkin in *Sea of Love.*

Similarly, *homme fatales* portray masculine dark-animus figures and seducers: Mickey Rourke's character in *9 ½ Weeks*, Cary Grant's in *Suspicion*, Robert Lowe's in *Masquerade*, and more demonic figures such as Dracula and Jack the Ripper. A less obvious shapeshifter is Al Pacino's character in *The Godfather* playing the role of the anti-hero who becomes a ruthless, cold-blooded, and unfeeling crime boss. His love interest, played by Diane

Keaton, realizes too late that his loyalty lies not with her but with the Corleone family legacy.

Practical function:
Awareness and assimilation of the anima and animus archetypes into your waking experience will allow more satisfying relationships and will also enhance emotions and abilities that currently lie dormant because of society's stereotypes about traditional male and female roles.

The man who becomes aware of the feminine psychological tendencies inside him and learns to accept them as truth instead of repressing these feelings elevates his station in life by accessing universal feminine qualities: feeling, intuition, prophetic hunches, receptiveness to the irrational, being in tune with nature, relation to the unconscious, and the capacity for personal love.

Likewise, the woman who becomes aware of the masculine psychological tendencies inside her and learns to accept them as truth instead of hiding these feelings elevates her station in life by accessing universal masculine qualities: objectivity, logical thinking, initiative, courage, assertiveness, drive, and an enterprising spirit.

TRICKSTER

The Cosmic Clown is the embodiment of the trickster archetype and is responsible for the energies of mischief, disruption, playfulness, and rebellious misconduct.

Psychological function:
Tricksters cut big egos down to size, rebel against the establishment and the status quo, point out hypocrisy, and bring heroes down to earth when they take themselves too seriously. Tricksters alert us when we have become stagnant. They point out the need for growth and change.

Dramatic function:
Introducing comic relief is a main dramatic function of tricksters. Too much tension, suspense, and serious conflict can become emotionally draining for the audience. Laughter is good medicine. In drama, tricksters also serve the same psychological functions of cutting down ego, making fun of the establishment, and shocking people to elicit change. Bugs Bunny, Daffy Duck, Charlie Chaplin, Jim Carey, Tom Green, Jerry Lewis, are all examples of playing trickster roles on screen.

Practical function:
The next time you encounter a trickster figure, whether in the media or in real-life, who does something shockingly distasteful or mischievous to make your blood boil, take a moment to calm down and exercise some patience. Tricksters expect you to lash out in anger. This is what they want. But you can turn the joke on them by practicing patience and tolerance.

Don't take life too seriously. Take time to have a good laugh. And if you find a trickster figure is getting on your nerves, it's a good time to reflect on why you are feeling hostile. Maybe it reminds you of a negative trait or dark secret about yourself that you have repressed and are not willing to admit to anyone. Or maybe you have become staid and stagnant in your ways and need to change.

SHADOW

As we covered in previous chapters, the shadow represents the dark side: our dark secrets, negative emotions, unexpressed feelings, repressed desires, unrealized wishes, emotional traumas, and all the stuff we don't like about ourselves that we aren't willing to admit to anyone, including ourselves. The shadow also represents raw, hidden energy that can be used for good or bad.

Psychological function:
If not acknowledged, confronted, and brought to awareness, the shadow becomes a destructive force with a life of its own causing us to form bad habits, do things we will live to regret, and even lead to psychoses. It often appears in our dreams as a monster or demon that haunts us.

Dramatic function:
The shadow's dramatic purpose is to annihilate the hero. Shadow figures bring out the best in heroes by introducing them to death or symbolic death. It forces the hero to rise to the challenge, defeat her opponent (her own demon or ego), and wear the crown of death. If the hero dies in her struggle, while fighting valiantly and sacrificing herself for a worthy cause or the liberation of her people, then she has earned her sleep in Elysium.

Practical function:
Know thyself! Understand your strengths and weaknesses, your desires and fears, your hopes and longings, where you begin and end. Choose your role in life: a hero, a villain, or nothing. If you choose to join the circle of herohood, then you must begin with three essential steps. All world religions teach it, yet few understand it. The Great One once said, "Deny yourself, take up your cross, and follow me." (Matthew 16:24) Jesus was talking about the great hero journey within:

THE HERO'S JOURNEY

1. **Deny Yourself**
2. **Take up your Cross**
3. **Follow Me**

1. Deny yourself. This has nothing to do with living an austere life and inflicting pain on one's self as many people are led to believe. It's about denying your *false* self. It's about looking inside at our ruinous pattern of sin (our dark thoughts, negative emotions, and unwarranted fears) and bringing it to light, our conscious awareness. A hero must annihilate his or her own ego. The ego is about ME! ME! ME! The soul is about We. By slaying the ego, your inner demons, you let the hero soul shine through. You must shed your old skin for a new you to emerge.

2. Take up your Cross. This is not about blindly accepting one's burdens in life and suffering silently. With ego out of the way, your soul shines brighter. That faint voice inside you, once barely audible, grows louder. Listen to your inner voice. It is your destiny. Become aware of your true potential, your calling. Do not be afraid. Do not deny the call for adventure. Accept your calling, your cross, with open heart and let your light shine. This is what is meant by taking up your cross. The hero journey begins.

3. Follow Me. Do not be deceived into thinking this is about being a follower, one who imitates without knowing, like a parrot. It's the opposite. It's about being your own leader and following your heart instead of your ego. It's about letting go and letting God. When you have taken up your cross and done all that you can, it's time to surrender to the Higher Power in you. Your Spirit is immortal. It is, was, and always will be. It is love omniscient. When you follow the greatest commandment of all, the one cosmic law called love, when you can learn to love even your worst enemy, then you will have arrived. You will have come full circle. The sword that slayed your ego, is the same sword that will knight you, and elevate you to a higher station in life. That sword is knowledge, which is wisdom, which is love.

WISDOM

"Nature is a glorious school for the heart! It is well; I shall be a scholar in this school and bring an eager heart to her instruction. Here I shall learn wisdom, the only wisdom that is free from disgust; here I shall learn to know God and find a foretaste of heaven in His knowledge. Among these occupations my earthly days shall flow peacefully along until I am accepted into that world where I shall no longer be a student, but a knower of wisdom."
– Ludwig Van Beethoven

The inscription at the entrance of the Greek Temple of Apollo at Delphi reads simply: "Know thyself." The ancient Greeks, who developed the very foundation of Western civilization as we know it today, understood the importance of self knowledge. The hero creed of ancient Greece was, "Know thyself, and you will know the gods and the universe." Knowledge, especially knowledge of self, is the genesis of wisdom. And yet, ignorance is all around us. We live in a society today that 'does not want to know.' Anything that smacks of wisdom, and the common retort is, "I don't want to know." Nobody wants to know! The phrase 'whatever' marks the psyche of our generation.

William Shakespeare, the greatest hero poet of all time, a man who elevated the hearts, minds, and souls of multitudes of nations, once stated, "Ignorance is the curse of God; knowledge is the wing where with we fly to heaven." Ignorance is not bliss. Ignorance is stupidity. We are prisoners of our own minds due to a lack of knowledge. Knowledge can serve to free our minds and enlighten our souls. Herohood begins from *wanting* to know; having an unquenchable thirst and desire for knowledge. "Wisdom begins in wonder," said Socrates. The ancient Greeks aspired to four pillars of knowledge: Science, Philosophy, the Arts, and Religion. The hero soul has a higher degree of awareness into these four pillars of knowledge. While heroes achieve mastery in at least one main area of calling, they are generalists in nature. They are 'Renaissance Heroes.' Heroes love to study the classics. Their broadmindedness and comprehensive understanding of life gives them depth of character, substance, and definition. They are electrifying, elevating, and charismatic. When a hero speaks, people listen because they sense that what a hero says is only the tip of the iceberg of what he knows.

There are many varying degrees of knowledge which we will explore in this chapter. Book knowledge, although highly useful as a tool for worldly advancement and achievement, is at the beginning stage of higher knowledge. Thinking, rationalizing, analyzing, and theorizing, hold their place at the lower rungs of wisdom.

Heroes don't spend a lot of time thinking and analyzing. They just act. Applied knowledge is far more superior. CEOs of very successful companies have the power to make decisions quickly. Business is made on decisions. Mediocre minds are never able to bring an idea or a dream into fruition because they think too much. By thinking too much, they eventually find a 'reason' why their idea is a bad idea, and why it won't work. Unfortunately, their ideas never leave the ground. The ideas lie there rotting away in the cobwebs of their mind. **DON'T THINK. ACT! ACT NOW!** Practice the hero's motto: "The place is here, the time is now."

Descartes once said, "I think, therefore I am." To that I would reply, "I think, therefore I am not!" I say this in jest, but truly, the mind is a donkey. Either you ride the donkey or the donkey will ride you. Most people do not have control over their minds. Their minds control them with conflicting thoughts, doubt, fear, whim, and fancy. The hero learns to discipline and control the mind - to direct it to their vision and purpose in life. The hero shuts the chatter of the mind, listening to the Divinity within. When Jesus chose to ride on a donkey to the holy city of Jerusalem, he did so intentionally as a symbolic act. I believe symbolically he was representing enlightenment through humility and control of the mind.

Above thinking, speaking, and reading are higher forms of knowledge including: instinctual knowledge, sexual or creative expression, emotional intelligence, intuition, self-expression or expression of truth, imagination, and divine wisdom. These higher forms of knowledge correspond with the seven chakras (energy centers of the human body) common in yoga or the seven churches of apocalypse mentioned in the bible in the chapter of Revelation.

The way of the hero's path is to illuminate these seven churches, chakras, energy centers, or associated endocrine glands within. By doing so, they awaken their superior senses and spiritual connection with God. For many people, these seven energy centers lie idle and their associated endocrine glands are atrophied. This is mainly because people don't breathe properly, don't exercise regularly, and eat too much junk food. All of the important endocrine glands and vital organs, such as the heart, lungs, kidneys, liver, pancreas, thyroid gland, sex glands, bladder, pituitary and pineal glands in the brain, all of these suffer from a lack of oxygen and stimulation that comes from deep breathing and regular exercise. To add insult to injury to the human machine, many people clog up their arteries with junk food that further blocks the flow of oxygen.

The hero, through regular exercise, plus practicing the disciplines of yoga, martial arts, tai chi, meditation, healthy eating habits, deep breathing from the diaphragm, and the seven virtues, illuminates the seven lamps within. This awakens the hero soul, and gives the hero incredible superpowers to achieve things most people only dream about. These are the same energy centers that the Bible mentions:

"Before the throne, seven lamps were blazing. These are the seven spirits of God." – Revelation 4:5 (The throne being the heavenly throne, nirvana, or enlightenment.)

Here is a listing of these seven 'lamps,' 'churches,' or 'chakras' in the context of yoga, and their associated higher forms of knowledge:

1st chakra – known as the base or root chakra, is located in the base of the spine and governs the kidneys and spinal column. Feelings of good health and connection to one's body originate from this energy center. Opening this chakra aids in awakening **instinct**.

2nd chakra – known as the sexual, sacral, or spleen chakra, governs the sex glands or spleen. Creativity, vitality, and **sexual expression** spring from this source.

3rd chakra – known as the solar plexus, situated in the abdominal cavity, behind the stomach and in front of the aorta, governs the pancreas, liver, spleen, stomach, gall bladder and the nervous system. This is the inferior emotional center of the human machine where emotional sense memory or **emotional intelligence** is absorbed. Opening this chakra also releases willpower, desire, self-respect, and confidence.

4th chakra – known as the heart chakra, governs the thymus gland, heart, blood, circulatory system and the immune and endocrine systems. The heart is the superior emotional center responsible for compassion and physical healing. Opening this chakra aids in **intuition.**

5th chakra – known as the throat chakra, or inner ear, governs the thyroid gland. It is responsible for communication or **self expression** - expression of truth and love. It also represents attunement with the music, vibration, or symphony of the universe where hearing and voice become one.

6th chakra – known as the third eye, in the middle of the forehead, governs the pituitary gland or lower brain. Opening this chakra awakens **imagination** or clairvoyance.

7th chakra – known as the Crown, the Lotus, or Christ Consciousness, governs the pineal gland or upper brain. This energy center is a combination of all that is. Opening this chakra leads to a deep spiritual connection with God. The Crown chakra acts as a bridge or umbilical cord between the human soul and divine spirit. It is divine knowledge or **inspiration**, the highest form of knowledge known to human beings. The pineal gland also has been known to activate the superior sense of creative willpower.

Let's briefly explore these seven superior forms of knowledge:

Instinct
Instinct aids the hero along his or her journey in surviving the physical realm. Our inferior basic instinct consists of

that raw 'fight or flight' response inherent in animal nature. Animals smell fear, and instantly attack anyone that is afraid. They usually attack the spine when they sense fear, as that is where the vibrations emanate from. Likewise, when they sense the threat of danger from an overpowering prey, they flee. When this sense is developed in heroes, they learn to avoid danger. A hero can sense when they walk in a room, or a hallway, if their life is going to be threatened in some way, and act accordingly. They literally will feel a chill going through their spine when danger lurks nearby. This is what Gavin De Becker calls "the gift of fear" in his book by the same title. Heroes immediately tune with their instinct and listen to what it tells them: don't breath, don't move, hide in a dark corner, play dead, make a loud noise, stare the opponent in the eye, run, fight, walk calmly, and so on. By having a highly developed instinct, the hero learns to avoid danger and violence. Violence that tragically many people become the unknowing victims of yet could have avoided.

Then there is the superior instinctual knowledge of being 'street wise.' Street smarts is the zeitgeist of being present, grounded, and in the moment. It comes from practicing one's craft or vocation in the real world and learning directly from the masters who have accomplished a great deal of success in the hero's field. Just by being in the presence of a successful mentor, the hero instinctively picks up success habits. On the streets, the hero acts and reacts instinctively without thinking.

Finally, the highest form of instinctual knowledge is the sense memory of our ancestors and the accumulated knowledge of all humanity. This knowledge is stored in the collective unconscious, portions of which are continually available to us in our dreams, in our stories, myths, and symbols, and through regular meditation.

Sexual Expression or Creativity

Heroes learn to find an appropriate medium for their sexual expression. They channel their sexual energy into creativity and vitality in their work, overcoming the shadow side of lust that can bring a hero down. When lovemaking with their partner, they invite Divinity into their experience. The sexual act becomes sacred and beautiful. Mutual feelings of passion, romance, and compassion light the soul on fire.

Heroes make time for a wonderful experience: taking a bath, lighting scented candles, listening to romantic music, reading poetry, arranging the bed with flowers, giving each other a sensual massage, caressing one another dearly. Whatever it is, they do it with patience, reverence, and care. Thus the joy and ecstasy of sex and love is prolonged. Instead of a 'dirty,' rushed, fleeting moment, it becomes a more enjoyable and enduring experience. In each other's arms, all sense of time is lost, as eternity is experienced.

"Stars, you are unfortunate, I pity you,
Beautiful as you are, shining in your glory,
Who guide seafaring men through stress and peril
And have no recompense from gods or mortals,
Love you do not, nor do you know what love is.
Hours that are aeons urgently conducting
Your figures in a dance through the vast heaven,
What journey have you ended in this moment,
Since lingering in the arms of my beloved
I lost all memory of you and midnight."

– Johann Wolfgang von Goethe, *Night Thoughts*

Emotional Intelligence

Self awareness is one of the highest aims a hero can ascribe to. Emotional intelligence ties into the theme of the hero creed, "know thyself." Emotional intelligence is a high degree of awareness of ones inner feelings. Daniel Goleman, the author who coined this term in his groundbreaking book, *Emotional Intelligence*, adeptly argues that a high IQ, or academic intelligence, does not guarantee success. In fact, I would argue that IQ plays a minor role in one's ability to live a good life. While we have given birth to a new millennium, society's view of human intelligence is still too narrow. Nothing less than a radical paradigm shift in thinking, a revolution in our collective awareness, is required for the evolution of our souls.

Heroes are keen observers of the subtle nuances of varying emotions stirring inside them. They take the time to ask themselves, "Why am I feeling this way? What's the root cause? How is it affecting me? Is this emotion productive for me at this time?" By being aware, heroes can effectively manage and direct their emotions. They are literally able to 'shake off' their bad moods in many instances. When a negative emotion such as anger begins to brew, they can check the emotion before it becomes destructive. Fear gone unchecked turns to anger. Anger turns to hatred. Hatred, in our violent society, can often take the form of rage; rage turns to blind fury. And fury leads to a path of destruction.

A lack of awareness of one's emotions can become incredibly dangerous. Being unconsciously swept away by negative emotions can generate severe depression or emotional outbursts that irreparably ruin marriages, partnerships, working relationships, and friendships. In more severe cases, it can lead to road rage, violence, suicide, and even murder.

The hero copes with these negative emotions by first of all becoming aware of them from the outset, and than exploring the root cause of the emotion. Perhaps they are feeling angry because they really feel hurt by rejection. Whatever the case may be, heroes are master re-framers: they view things from a different perspective and look at alternatives. For example, in the case of rejection, they consider the possibility that the other person may be feeling hurt and rejected themselves from a past experience. Or simply, that the person might be having a really bad day. In any case, they don't view the perceived rejection as personal. From a business standpoint, especially in sales, heroes will not only reframe, but will adopt an entirely new belief system such as, "massive rejection equals massive success." This is not just a cute saying, but a hard-knocks fact: more "no's" lead to more "yes's" and more sales.

Heroes, being Warriors of Excellence, go way beyond just understanding their own emotions. They are keen observers of other people's emotions as well. By being able to perceive the changing tides of emotion in other people, they are able to penetrate the depths of their souls. When other people are experiencing the basic emotions of fear, anger, love, surprise, disgust, or sadness heroes tune in and absorb the emotions into their system.

These basic emotions, like the basic colors, can be combined to form thousands of nuances of emotions such as contentment, joy, horror, melancholy, lust, greed, frustration, disappointment, euphoria, envy, pride, humility, confidence, courage, fury, vengeance, arrogance, industry, etc. By paying attention, listening, empathizing, studying the facial features and pace of movements, and looking into the eyes of people, heroes are able to increase their emotional intelligence or understanding of other people. In so doing, the hero has access to a much wider range of emotions in effectively relating and dealing with people. One cannot be a great leader without thoroughly understanding human emotions and their underlying motivations.

Intuition

Intuition is direct knowledge without thinking. It is the power of knowing or understanding something immediately without reasoning. Where the solar plexus acts as the entry point for emotions, serving as an antenna that transmits and receives emotional waves, the heart is like the store house of emotions; which is why it is also often called the emotional center or seat of the soul. The heart is the universal symbol of love, the deepest of human emotions. Intuition, the ability to divine the possibilities of the unseen, resides in the heart.

Heroes have highly developed powers of intuition, because they are in tune with their hearts. With a quick glance they can get a snapshot panoramic perception of all that is at any given moment. With intuition, they are able to perceive a multitude of sensory queues around them at the same time: the gentle whisper of the wind, a falling leaf, a hesitant glance by a stranger in the distance, a sign on a truck passing by, a subtle vibration in the ground below, a shadow in the dark, an executive about to make an important decision. All of these queues combine to form an immediate knowledge that the hero acts on.

These experiences are what people call a hunch or a gut feeling. For many people, these moments are few and far between. The ability to instantly act on these 'hunches' is even rarer still. All too often, that special moment of perception becomes an afterthought, and opportunity slips away, never to be seen again. Gone. In a flash! The woman or man of your dreams smiles at you and walks away in the rush hour crowd. Responding to a phone number on a passing truck could have led to your biggest account. The man wearing a t-shirt and blue jeans in the coffee shop, takes a longer than usual glance at the book you are reading, then gets back to reading his paper. He could have financed your business idea. But your nose is still in your book. Eventually you finish your coffee, and leave without a conversation. If you don't use your intuition, countless opportunities will pass you by.

Because heroes are deeply in tune with their hearts, they act on these intuitive experiences that guide them in their quest for truth. The ancient Egyptians believed every human being had a god living within his or her heart. This is why during mummification, or embalming a dead body, the Egyptians removed all internal organs, leaving only the heart in place. I believe the Egyptians were right in their wisdom that divinity resides in the heart. Just close your eyes, look within, and put your hand on your heart. Listen to the beating of your heart, and you will hear the beautiful symphony of the universe! Listen to your heart in silence and you will begin developing your powers of intuition. In time, you will be able to hear an inner guiding voice that springs from the divine in you.

Self-expression

Beethoven once declared, "Music is a higher revelation than philosophy... Music, verily, is the mediator between intellectual and sensuous life...the one incorporeal entrance into the higher world of knowledge which comprehends mankind but which mankind cannot comprehend."

He was talking about the music of eternity. The symphony of the universe that lies in our hearts and dwells in everything around us: rivers, oceans, rocks, trees, and all of nature and the entire cosmos. Beethoven was a genius not only because he could hear this inner voice, but because he could also communicate it with such truth and passion.

This is synonymous with 'finding one's voice.' In eastern disciplines such as yoga, this is attained from connecting with the throat chakra or center of expression, which controls the ears and vocal chords, and tuning with the heart.

Listen to the music of your heart and do not be afraid to communicate truthfully. Pay careful attention to the range of emotions in your heart. Put your hand on your heart and listen to the symphony – the vibration and dance of creation. Listen in silence as a serene, frozen pond listens, and you will tune with your inner voice.

When you have learned to do this and can communicate genuinely from your heart, amazing things begin to happen. When you are willing to risk rejection and vulnerability by communicating deep from within your heart, the universe unfolds with love. People respond more openly to your voice and have a strong urge to help fulfill the desires of your heart in any way they can. Whether it's a friend, a loved one, a coworker, or a relative, you project truth. And truth has the power to set people free.

Even within professional, corporate settings, truth and love that come from the heart always win out over the intellect. If you are making a sales or business presentation, you will more likely win over the audience by speaking from your gut rather than spewing out overly intellectualized features. Winston Churchill did not say, "Never, never, have an unbalanced portfolio." Martin Luther King Jr. did not say, "I have a step-by-step leadership strategy." When you speak boldly from the depths of your heart and soul, people will be moved, motivated, and truly inspired.

Imagination

Imagination is knowledge about reality without being there. Imagination is one of the most creative and powerful forces available to the hero. The lowest form of imagination involves simply imagining in the mind's eye what can already be seen. It is synonymous to making a 'xerox copy' of an original idea. The highest form of imagination is clairvoyance, which is the ability to see events or objects that cannot be perceived by the five senses. That is why imagination, in its highest form, is often called the *sixth sense*.

With imagination an Olympic athlete can picture herself finishing the race first and winning the gold medal - the national anthem playing, the flag raised, the flaming torch above, the crowd cheering in the background, and tears of glorious triumph streaming down her trembling face - all before it even happens. With imagination, the NBA pro basketball champion can visualize himself throwing a thousand practice shots, perfectly each and every time. With time, all the muscles in his body have adjusted themselves to match a winning performance, by imagination alone! All the neural pathways become etched in his brain, programmed for winning. Victory becomes inevitable.

The great poet can use all the faculties of imagination to transport himself to the city of Paris under a brilliant moonlit sky without having to go there physically. The master sculptor can see the beauty that lies within what others can only see as a plain slab of marble. And the skilful writer can carry us to new unexplored worlds and fantastic adventures. Such is the power of imagination: to see the unseen, to chart the uncharted territory, to dream the undreamed! Imagination is creative because it gives us power to create. And thus, we become co-creators of our own destiny.

Inspiration or divine knowledge

Webster's Dictionary defines inspiration as, "a divine influence or action on a person believed to qualify him or her to receive *and* communicate sacred revelation." Inspiration is divine knowledge inhaled. I truly believe inspiration is the voice of God, or the Genius Within, compelling us to create. Beethoven, Bach, Mozart, John Lennon, Helen Keller, Marie Curie, Anne Frank, Maria Callas, Shakespeare, Muhammad, Jesus, Buddha, Gandhi, Martin Luther King Jr., all were inspired by Divinity. It is inherent in the very definition of inspiration itself. It is one thing to receive 'sacred revelation,' and quite another to communicate it effectively. Great heroes do both. They elevate the souls of the masses by projecting their divine inspiration outward onto humanity.

Of all the forms of knowledge, divine knowledge is the highest. Divine knowledge is a combination of all the forms of knowledge and can be obtained by activating all seven energy centers in the body. To reach this state of awareness one has to fall in love with knowledge. Inspiration is a direct connection to God. To make this connection one first has to awaken their soul, which is the bridge between the human machine and the Spirit. By raising the level of awareness or consciousness of their thoughts (the head), combined with a high degree of awareness of their emotions (the heart), the hero awakens his or her soul.

Nelson Mandela once said, "A good head and a good heart are always a formidable combination." It is absolutely essential for putting the soul back into politics and economics – infusing life into our dead society. Awakening the soul requires one to be in love with knowledge. The soul is knowledge, plus knowledge, plus knowledge. It is a hunger to know. This is why creative willpower is so closely connected with inspiration and the soul. (In yoga, creative willpower is harnessed from activating the pineal gland in the upper brain often associated with the seventh chakra.)

There is a distinction between the willpower that resides in the solar plexus and heart, the inferior and superior emotional centers respectively, and *creative* willpower. Willpower is like the 'Raging Bull.' It is raw emotion that overwhelms us with an overpowering drive to do something, to overcome, to rise above, and to achieve. But the wise person quickly realizes that in order to achieve any aim, they need more and more knowledge. It's like playing golf. Amateurs are stuck in their raw emotion to achieve. They end up trying too hard to hit the ball and swinging too hard with little results. Professional golf players through knowledge of the sport, learn to excel by relaxing and swinging through the ball with ease. Willpower serves only as an impetus. Raw emotion, like a diamond in the rough, has to be refined, polished, and honed properly to achieve perfection. The hero must symbolically tame or slay the raging bull.

Creative willpower is the soaring Cosmic Eagle of our souls rising effortlessly above mountains to gain a higher perspective. Creative willpower is the desire and determination to gain more and more knowledge. It is the highest form of willpower. With eagle perspective, we see the grand vision enfolding within us. Through applied knowledge we project our inner vision outwardly, and the universe responds to our vision by making our dreams a reality.

A lot of people think they can instantly 'light up' all seven lamps within and gain immediate wisdom. But this is as ridiculous as thinking that by one day doing a 100 push-ups, one will be fit for life. Life does not work that way. You have to work at it every day. It takes time and patience. There is no crash course on wisdom. The Bible puts it very simply in Job 12:12, "With the ancient is wisdom; and in length of days, understanding."

And how does one become wise? With time, knowledge, love, patience, meditation, prayer, and experience, one gains wisdom. You must be in love with knowledge twenty-four hours a day. Know thyself and you will know the gods. For wisdom, at its highest, is divine knowledge.

Heroes also know that one of the fastest ways of gaining wisdom or divine knowledge is by studying and applying the timeless principles found in every religion. Many people are fed up with religion. They think religion is a fanatical approach to controlling people. They are wrong. They think religion causes wars and strife among people. They are wrong. People are the cause of war and hatred, because of their ignorance or lack of knowledge, not religion. Most people today have no clue what religion really means.

The word religion comes from the Latin root 're-ligare,' which means to re-connect. To re-connect with what? To re-connect with the Spirit! We are disconnected individuals. Most people are disconnected with God. Their minds are disconnected from the Spirit. They are disconnected from the place where dreams are born and where healing begins. This is why so many people are physically and mentally ill. And this is why drugs and psychotherapy are big business.

We have forgotten what it means to be human. We are not human! We only think we are. Human derives its roots from the ancient term hu-manas. Hu means spirit, and manas means mind. The roots can be traced back even before Latin to ancient Chinese, Sufi, Tibetan, and Sanskrit languages. To be human literally means to have mind and spirit bound together as one. Our minds are disconnected from the Spirit. We need to re-connect. Studying and practicing religion allows the hero to go deeper and deeper into truth, thus gaining enlightened wisdom. All heroes are 'religious.' They just choose to call their ways by different names: spiritual, genius, god-inspired, creative, charismatic, healer, enlightened, or whatever buzzword society feels comfortable with at the time.

At the peak of awareness one begins to understand the concept of Trinity as One. It is a difficult concept to understand: how can the Father, the Son, and the Holy Ghost be one and the same? And yet they are one. Just as love, soul, and wisdom are one. The soul is knowledge plus knowledge plus knowledge. It is awareness of ones thoughts combined with awareness of one's feelings. That is true wisdom. Wisdom is divine knowledge. With wisdom one can see the Divinity within every human being and thus have compassion and love for all. Wisdom is love and love is wisdom. They are One.

Heroes are not 'good'- they are wise. They are not naive and so cannot be fooled or taken advantage of easily. This is because heroes have a higher degree of awareness of themselves, of others, of nature, of life, and of the Spirit. Don't be 'good,' be wise. Don't be a nice guy, be a Wise Guy. Be a Wise Gal.

COURAGE

"Courage is being scared to death - but saddling up anyway."
– John Wayne

Courage is the cliché hallmark attributed to the hero. I say cliché because people talk about courage as if it is some mysterious force only a hero is born with. Courage is a vague and fleeting concept for many people because they lack it themselves. People lack courage because they lack knowledge. They have no idea where the true source of courage comes from. Even worse, they don't know it and continue to live in fear. As Socrates pointed out, "People not only don't know, but they don't know that they don't know."

This is why so many people on earth live in fear. Fear of death. Fear of life. Fear of living their nightmares. And fear of living their dreams. Most people are followers because they lack self-confidence and live in constant fear. Anyone who is brave and can show them how to overcome fear, they follow and respect. But God forbid, anyone that reminds people of their own fear, they attack and abuse viciously! This is human nature in its lowest, animal form.

What is fear? Fear is the perception or misperception of the unknown. Perception of how we negatively view reality, but not reality itself. I once heard somewhere, a useful acronym for FEAR: False Evidence that Appears Real. The 'false evidence' being our own manufactured worries, doubts, and negative images often of events that haven't even taken place yet. William Shakespeare understood this principal well when he said, "Our doubts are traitors, and make us lose the good we oft might win, by fearing to attempt."

The cause of fear is lack of knowledge. Therefore, 'knowledge is the antidote to fear' according to the great American hero philosopher, Ralph Waldo Emerson. That is why heroes are brave souls. They immerse themselves with knowledge, plus knowledge, plus knowledge. Heroes know that they don't know, but are willing to learn. They are humble and learn from everyone regardless of rank or status. Leaders *know* their potential. Followers ignore their potential. Courage and self-confidence comes from knowledge and self-knowledge.

But where does knowledge come from? This is where most books on leadership fall short. God is the direct source of all knowledge. The stars, the cosmos, our solar system and all the planets, nature, the human soul, all come from the Divine. The hero gains courage by drawing on a Higher Power. Heroes have a strong, spiritual faith in the Infinite Network. They let go and let God, realizing they are but a conduit, a channel for Divine expression. Emptying their minds, they surrender to the spiritual power which flows through them like a bursting dam. With faith, all things are made possible. Fear melts away in the presence of God and one can move mountains!

Studying religion provides insights and lessons to the hero soul about effectively dealing with fear, worry, anxiety, depression, and other afflictions of the mind. Religion provides a door into the unknown. Also, praying in times of worry and trouble helps the hero heal and cope with fear.

This being said, no human hero is entirely fearless. Great heroes are not born fearless and brave. Nelson Mandela had this to say about courage: "I learned that courage was not the absence of fear, but the triumph over it...I felt fear myself more times than I can remember, but I hid it behind a mask of boldness. The brave man is not he who does not feel afraid, but he who conquers that fear." By asking God directly for help and guidance, heroes are able to conquer fear and act in spite of it. And when death smiles upon them, they smile back.

THE WAY OF THE HERO

"The cliché about the game being you against the golf course is only partly true. Ultimately, it is you against yourself. It always comes down to how well you know yourself, your ability, your limitations and the confidence you have in your ability to execute under pressure that is mostly self-created. Ultimately, you must have the *heart* and *head* to play a shot and the *courage* to accept the consequences."
– Tiger Woods, *How I Play Golf*

The Head, the Heart, and Courage. This is the way of the hero. In some of my fondest childhood memories, I can clearly recall the story of Dorothy's magical journey in the children's classic *The Wizard of Oz*. In the Land of Oz, Dorothy encounters three archetypes: the Scarecrow, who needs a brain to *think*, the Tin Man, who needs a heart to *feel*, and the Lion, who needs the *courage* to act. And Dorothy needs to find her way home. Together they go on a remarkable and scary adventure in search of the great Wizard of Oz, who they falsely believe can restore balance and return what's missing in their lives.

L. Frank Baum, the original author of *The Wonderful Wizard of Oz* (1900), from which the classic movie was based on, was a genius. He really understood the path of herohood and was able to poetically communicate his vision in the form of a fable that everyone could relate to. As is always the case for the hero starting out, his work was initially shunned because people in power could not understand, or more likely, were simply not willing to understand. Frank's book was banned for several years, because librarians felt it was not 'important' juvenile literature. But there may have been a hidden agenda for the banning of the book. It is possible that the intellectual elite, who were predominantly all male at the time, felt threatened by the fact that the protagonist, Dorothy, was a female hero.

Frank believed that with faith we all have the power to live our dreams. He was probably motivated from his own longings and weaknesses. Ironically, Frank was born with a faulty, weak heart. This limited his participation in any strenuous activity. As a result, he was a frail and timid child who lacked self-confidence in social situations.

However, his powerful faith and vivid imagination, more than made up for his weak heart and frailty. Frank did a lot of daydreaming as a kid. He used his imagination to penetrate the darkness of his world and to behold a vision. He used the power of his faith to come back home and share his vision.

Frank's vision unfolded in the form of a classic children's tale that clearly outlined the complete path of the hero's journey: 1. Losing consciousness, denying self, or willed introversion, 2. Confronting one's unconscious fears, clarifying them, or slaying the Ego, 3. Breaking on through to the other side where dreams are born, where one finds one's calling and surrenders to the Force, and 4. Returning home, renewed and transformed, to share their vision or teach the enlightening lesson they have learned.

This is the path that every classic hero, whether mythic or real, has undertaken along their journey. It is the very same journey that Shamans, renowned psychologists such as Jung and Freud, and great religious leaders such as Jesus, Buddha, and Muhammad have lead their people through to experience transformation and healing.

Dorothy followed the very same hero path: she lost consciousness and went within through her nightmare, she confronted her inner most fears, witches, and demons, she went 'over the rainbow' to the other side, and finally, she came back home, renewed, to share her lesson. L. Frank Baum, couldn't have simplified the hero journey any further. It was one of the few successful female hero journeys ever to be depicted in a children's book and in Hollywood at that time.

And what was Dorothy's lesson? One does not need to travel the ends of the earth seeking false prophets to find oneself. The Wizard is an imposter. There is no Wizard. Only God within. The answer lies within. Don't 'follow the yellow brick road' like a herd of blind sheep. Take the road less traveled and look within. Having faith in one's higher Self, which lies within, is all one needs to find oneself.

In the case of the Scarecrow, the Tin Man, and the Lion, they each thought they were missing something vital: intellect, feeling, and courage. And so, they went on a long, exhausting quest to find the Wizard of Oz, who they thought could solve their problems and restore what was missing. Of course, they were sadly disappointed to learn that the Great Wizard was the Great Imposter. He was a real shyster.

But they soon realized that the qualities they so desperately longed for, already resided within themselves. They only needed to search deeper within themselves. In the end, the Wizard rewarded them with outward symbols of success for the qualities they already had within and unknowingly demonstrated along their journey. The Scarecrow receives an 'honorary degree in Th.D' (Doctor of Thinkology). The Tin Man is awarded with a big, red, heart-shaped, tick-tocking clock. And the Lion is presented with a Medal of Valor.

Even Dorothy realizes at the end that she no longer needs the help of the Good Witch of the North. She already has the power to go back home to Kansas. You see, many of us act like that miserable, whimpering, cowardly lion in *The Wizard of Oz*. This is because we live in a wimpy world. People are raised in a society that is afraid of the truth. Few people seek the truth, and thus we live in ignorance.

We are lions in sheep's clothing, wandering around aimlessly, *baaahing* and following the herd. Many people have lived all their lives *among* sheep and raised *as* sheep, that they believe they *are* sheep. But sometimes they get separated from the herd. In their new surroundings they feel a deep yearning inside. They call out. But instead of *baaahing*, they roar. Realize that you are a lion. Return to the lion's den and reclaim your natural thrown.

THE HERO HEART

"The chemist who can extract from his heart's elements, compassion, respect, longing, patience, regret, surprise, and forgiveness and compound them into one can create that atom which is called love."
– Kahlil Gibran

The hero has a kind heart. A warm, compassionate, and caring heart. A tender heart, overflowing with love. This is the hero heart; the heart of the peaceful warrior. For the hero is a gentle tiger: ferocious, magnificent, and strong, yet kind-hearted. He is dangerous and feared, but also respected, because he has love and compassion in his heart.

When one has control of their heart, they have the key to unlock some of the mysteries of the universe. New doors open that were never seen before, leading to hidden treasures. Along the hero's journey, old hags and ugly toads will appear to test the hero soul. The gentle soul with a kind and generous heart will open up like a budding rose to kiss the twilight dew of dawn. And through giving, the hero will heal herself, by healing others.

In his autobiography, *Long Walk to Freedom*, Nelson Mandela mentioned this aspect of the hero heart by telling his readership the tale of a great African Xhosa Legend: "[There was a] traveler who was approached by an old woman with terrible cataracts on her eyes. The woman asked the traveler for help, and the man averted his eyes. Then another man came along and was approached by the old woman. She asked him to clean her eyes, and even though he found the task unpleasant, he did as she asked. Then miraculously, the scales fell from the old woman's eyes and she became young and beautiful. The man married her and became wealthy and prosperous. 'It is a simple tale, but its message is an enduring one: virtue and generosity will be rewarded in ways that one cannot know.'"

Joseph Campbell, in his uplifting book, *The Hero With A Thousand Faces,* writes about the adventures of Huang Ti, the 'Yellow Emperor' (2697-2597 B.C.), the first Emperor of China, who learns about the mysteries of the heart in a vision. Joseph Campbell cites from Herbert A. Giles' work, *A Chinese Biographical Dictionary*: "[Huang Ti's] distinguishing endowment was his power to dream. In sleep he could visit the remotest regions and consort with immortals in the supernatural realm. In his dream that lasted 3 months...he learned the lesson of the control of the heart....He instructed them in the control of the forces of nature in their own hearts."

There is something quite remarkable in the continued fascination with the human heart throughout history. There must be some powerful, mysterious force, an extraordinary wisdom that resides in the heart for it to be recognized as the universal symbol of love. I believe a special intelligence resides in the heart; so much so, that the heart could be called the human machine's second brain.

Aristotle, and even the ancient Egyptians, believed the heart was the acropolis or central regulatory body. Scientists have of course discovered since then, that the brain is the central regulatory body. However, I don't believe the ancients, who studied science, medicine, and anthropology more intensely, were too far off in their thinking. After all, the heart does supply blood to all parts of the body, including the brain. We know that the heart has bundles of nerve endings. Only recently in human history have scientists discovered that the heart is no mere pump, but also an endocrine gland. Aside from relatively being geographically centered within the body, the ancients understood something about the heart that is far deeper in its wisdom; something very mysterious, that we still cannot fully understand. Something so powerful, and yet simple, that science cannot measure or even fathom.

For the beating of the heart is the beating of time. The heart is in perfect synchronicity with the rhythm of the universe. It is the dance of the cosmos and the song of the divine. Listen to the heart and the mysteries of the universe unfold. Yogis, Tibetan monks, and ancient sages of the East have understood this principle for thousands of years. It is only recently becoming more widely known in the West as the world grows smaller.

Spiritual leaders from the East, such as Deepak Chopra and the Dalai Lama, are bringing these findings to the West. Deepak Chopra, who was heralded by Time Magazine as one of the top 100 heroes and icons of the 21st century, understood the healing and guiding power of the heart. In his best-selling book, *The Seven Spiritual Laws of Success*, Dr. Chopra says, "I will then ask my heart for guidance and be guided by its message of comfort or discomfort. If the choice feels comfortable, I will plunge ahead with abandon. If the choice feels uncomfortable, I will pause and see the consequences of my action with my inner vision. This guidance will enable me to make spontaneously correct choices for myself and for all those around me."

By learning to shut the mind and tune with the heart, we can make more effective decisions that will move us toward our dreams more frequently. This is because our deepest desires lie within our hearts. And our desires come from the Divine. The word desire comes from the Latin root de – sire, meaning 'of the Father.' And so, I believe the ancients were right in their belief that divinity dwells in the heart. Empty your mind of all thoughts and listen to your heart in beautiful silence. Even the Bible says,

"...When you are on your beds, search your hearts and be silent." (Psalm 4:4) The Divine voice will speak, and guide you along your hero path.

The Chicago Bulls basketball legend, Michael Jordan, was once asked by an interviewer, "If you had to put a team around you, what's the one quality you'd want?" Michael Jordan replied, "Heart. That would be the biggest thing. I think heart means a lot. It separates the great from the good players." [Taken from *Playboy's* May '92 Interview]

RESPECT

"I always believed in love, compassion, and a sense of universal respect. Every human being has that potential."
– The Dalai Lama

Respect is the foundation of love. Without respect there is no love. How can one even begin to love if they have no respect for themselves? How can one say, "I love you," without respecting the other person? Love is impossible without respect!

Talking about respect is easy. Practicing it is very difficult because it involves humility. One must lose one's ego to become truly humble. Ego is ME! ME! ME! The soul is WE. One must put the ego to sleep, and awaken the soul. Then, and only then, can we see the potential in every human being.

When ego is annihilated, we see the Divinity in all. The greatest feat a hero can accomplish is to journey into the darkness of his or her unconscious and slay the ego with one swift blow. The hero can then develop a sense of universal respect: respect for nature, respect for life, respect for death, respect for the genius within, and respect for all beings - including the enemy.

How can we possibly respect our enemies, people who have betrayed, scorned, and violated us? It starts with humility and understanding. By following the pain, to see the hurt behind the mask of hatred in the enemy's eyes, we can realize that we too are capable of evil. By penetrating the soul of our enemy, we can glimpse a ray of hope within. We don't necessarily have to like our enemies, but we can respect them. Only then can we learn to love them and heal ourselves. For the real enemy lies within us.

Nelson Mandela, a man who suffered years of cruelty and injustice in the hands of his enemies, was still able to see a ray of hope in humanity. In his autobiography, he wrote:

"I always knew that deep down in every human heart, there is mercy and generosity. No one is born hating another person because of the color of his skin, or his background, or his religion. People must learn to hate, and if they can learn to hate, they can be taught to love, for love comes more naturally to the human heart than its opposite. Even in the grimmest times in prison, when my comrades and I were pushed to the limits, I would see a glimmer of humanity in one of the guards, perhaps just for a second, but it was enough to reassure me and keep me going. Man's goodness is a flame that can be hidden but never extinguished."

THE UNDERWORLD

"The roaring of lions, the howling of wolves, the raging of the stormy sea, and the destructive sword, are portions of eternity too great for the eye of man."
– William Blake, *The Marriage of Heaven and Hell*

The story of Perseus, the legendary Greek hero and son of Zeus, is the hyper-myth classic heroic journey into the underworld and safe return. According to Carlos Parada's work, *Genealogical Guide to Greek Mythology*, Perseus was bound into a chest with his mother as her illegitimate child and cast into the sea. Washing up on the shores of the island of Seriphus, Perseus was immediately given the difficult task of bringing the head of Gorgon Medusa to the king.

Medusa was once a beautiful maiden who, in her foolish pride and vain glory, dared to compare herself to the goddess Athena. Medusa was said to have been ravished in Athena's own temple by Poseidon, the Greek god who had dominion over the seas. This defilement infuriated Athena and she destroyed Medusa's beauty, turning her into a frightfully ugly monster. Medusa's beautiful ringlets of hair, once her pride and joy, were turned into hissing serpents.

Medusa became a cruel, horrific monster who took pleasure in torturing her victims. According to legend, her aspect was so frightening that anyone that laid eyes on her turned to stone. But her reign of terror was soon brought to an end by Perseus who was aided by the gods. He was given a silver shield by Athena, winged sandals by the god Hermes, and a helmet that would make its wearer invincible by the god Hades.

In the darkness, Perseus approached the sleeping Medusa. Wearing Hades' helmet, he was rendered invisible. Through his cunning, Perseus slew Medusa by looking at her reflection in his shield, cutting off her head and putting it in his magic purse. From Medusa's beheaded, teeming neck sprang the winged Pegasus, who flew away into the skies and entered heaven.

With Medusa's enraged, two immortal Gorgon sisters in pursuit of him, Perseus took flight and escaped with the aide of Hermes winged sandals and Hades helmet. Upon returning, he presented Medusa's head to Athena, who placed the head into the center of her shield the Aegis.

This is such a fascinating hero tale of the journey within, into the dark night of the soul, and return, that there is beauty in its very horror. The wolves, the ogres, the hags, the dragons, the serpents, the Gorgons, the Cyclops, the demons, the monsters, the witches - all these denizens of the underworld are frightful to behold. They evoke terror, yet are thrilling to challenge and defeat. We are made drunk by the shedding of their blood. And in our sweet intoxication of death, new celestial heights encountered.

There are as many interpretations of ancient Greek mythology as there are people on this planet. My interpretation focuses more on the psychological journey of the hero's quest. In my view, Perseus was slaying himself; his own ugly, distorted ego. By descending into the unconscious realm that defines his character, he dies to the world without, to be reborn within – transcending the known into the unknown.

In the valley of death, Perseus encounters his hidden fears, and meets his dark prince. By shattering his own ego, he frees the beautiful, captive soul within. I believe this is symbolized in Perseus' act of slaying Medusa. The winged Pegasus that emerges from within Medusa's slain body, flying into the skies above, represents the freedom of his once trapped soul. This is a common human theme that echoes through many fables around the world. Stories such as Jonah trapped in the belly of the whale for three days and three nights, or the mean wolf swallowing Little Red Riding Hood reflect this motif. Little Red Riding Hood representing our trapped soul, while the wolf, our ego. Once the wolf is slain, and its belly torn open, the soul is set free.

An interesting distinction should be made, however, in Perseus' journey into the underworld and escape: upon slaying his inner demon, he took flight without passing through the gates leading to the 'other side' of darkness, into the city of light. He did not enter into that heavenly state of pure bliss, where the ultimate boon of unlimited possibilities exists. Notice that he did not mount the winged Pegasus and fly off into heaven. Perseus followed the more common hero journey of encountering a great inner fear, overcoming it, and than returning to his people with a lesson.

Perseus was not prepared to deal with the enormous power of divine truth. He simply was not ready and did not have the skill or capacity to handle such knowledge. It would have overwhelmed him. For the forces of the dark abyss are not to be defied and challenged lightly. Willed introversion and losing all sense of consciousness, without proper training and experience, can have dire effects. A prolonged stay within the realm of the underworld can lead to paranoia, schizophrenia, neurosis, and psychosis. One faces the danger of being trapped in a permanent trance where reality and illusion become blurred.

But the hero who has developed the emotional, physical, mental, and spiritual muscle, can fully penetrate this wall of darkness with the proper training, skill, knowledge, and experience. This bursting of the universal bubble releases a flood of spiritual energy that blesses the hero with divine knowledge and the titanic powers to enlighten and elevate entire civilizations.

The Prophet Muhammad's life is symbolic of reaching such a stage of enlightenment. In the famous 'Ascension' dream known in Islam as the Miraj or 'Stairway to Heaven,' the Prophet Muhammad mounted the magical winged horse of fire, Burak (the Horse of Abraham), and ascended to Heaven. This dream that took place in the year of 621 became the foundation of the Islamic faith. [*The Bokhari*, Vol. 15, 3615] Similarly, the birth, death, and resurrection of Jesus Christ became the foundation of the Christian faith.

From this state of divine bliss, the hero breaks through personal limitations and realizes that he or she is one with the universe. It is then that the duality of good and evil is understood. One finally realizes that the same light that creates also destroys. That mother and father are but one reflection of each other. In this field of spontaneous potentiality, the hero realizes that he or she is truly creative. And in this moment the hero becomes one with the Cosmic Creator. All things become possible.

"This is thy hour O Soul, thy free flight
      into the wordless,
Away from books, away from art, the day
      erased, the lesson done,
Thee fully forth emerging, silent, gazing,
      Pondering the themes thou lovest best,
Night, sleep, death and the stars."

– Walt Whitman, *Leaves of Grass*

THE AWAKENING

"Behold, the Kingdom of God is within you."
– Jesus (Luke 17:21)

Lying dormant at the bottom of the deep seas of our subconscious is the lost City of Atlantis. Within the abyss of nothingness and silence, it lies submerged in total darkness. The hero's mission is to awaken this source of light reflection, and thus awaken our soul. The time has come to raise the lost City of Atlantis. The City of Light.

When we look in the mirror we see our reflection looking back. For most people, this reflection is a reflection of who they are entirely. This is the illusion that most people live by day in and day out. The reality is that this image we see before us is but a reflection of light bouncing off particles in space. Who is the grand master puppeteer behind the image that controls our actions, emotions, and thoughts? Where does our creativity and deepest desires spring from? Who dreams our dreams for us? Who gives us the imagination to transport us from past, present, and future?

These are the questions a hero ponders along his or her quest. When the hero develops the courage and capacity to slay his inner demons, serpents, dragons, witches, ogres, and monsters that guard his double, he is then able to see a whole new universe that lies submerged: the lost City of Atlantis. It is a parallel universe of pure light. The hero sees himself as the entire cosmos, realizing every particle is intelligent, the billions of atoms with their whirling masses of electrons and protons, solar systems onto themselves, whirling into galaxies, themselves whirling into one massive, revolving circle of eternity. It is then the hero re-unites with his double, the dreamer of his dreams, his ultimate maker. The hero experiences at-one-ment with the Father.

This is the 'Great Awakening,' the revolution of the soul. It represents the transformation from unconscious to conscious, from ego to soul, darkness to light. It is the spiritual redemption and regeneration of the soul where the hero experiences God within. When the mind and spirit are reconnected, the City of Light emerges.

Spirit is the energy that animates matter. Jesus' act of turning water into wine can be interpreted symbolically to represent the water of the human machine transformed into the wine of spirit. It is the universal act of becoming human: spiritualizing the human machine. It is the miracle of being born again, becoming alive, multidimensional, and comprehensive. When we spiritualize the human machine, our inferior self dissolves and ego shatters.

The shattering of the universal bubble is like the splitting of an atom of the mind, unleashing an incredible explosion of new power. The explosion sets off a chain reaction that affects people around the globe. Like a stack of dominoes everything falls into place to carry out the hero's mission. It is from this place, that one's deepest desires are easily met. It is like an avalanche of abundance, a torrent of blessings and unlimited wealth that result from universal cooperation.

The penetration of darkness into light, opening the doors between the known and the unknown, causes a tremendous torrent of unleashed creativity and energy unparalleled. From this awakening, great masterpieces, classics, symphonies, and inventions are born. The power can sometimes be so intense, so great in its magnitude, that one hero can shape the destiny of an entire civilization.

Indeed, this was the case with Huang Ti, the legendary ancient Chinese ruler known as the Yellow Emperor. He was known throughout world history as the founder of

Chinese civilization, accomplishing such enormous feats as fathering the Chinese language, authoring the first Chinese medical text, building the Great Wall of China, and engineering the social and political unification of the Chinese Empire. Perhaps one day, Albert Einstein may go down in history, as the man who helped shape the destiny, not only of a civilization, but of the world.

In the case of Huang Ti, some people believe he was guided by alien intelligent life forms, or was an extraterrestrial himself to have accomplished so much in such a short time span. A similar view is held by many people regarding the building of the ancient pyramids.

The hero soul encounters spiritual guides along the journey. When a hero is in tune with her soul, guides will appear. It may be actual people in life (an old man or woman, a child, a stranger), or it may be the supernatural spirit guides that the hero meets when she journeys into the darkness of her deep subconscious mind through dreams and visions.

A more advanced hero would have the capacity to go deeper and deeper, beyond the subconscious mind, to penetrate the darkness, entering the City of Light, on the other side. The penultimate hero is able to survive this experience, still awake, and bring back to the people this sacred knowledge, fully intact.

Sometimes heroes need to be aided along the way. I believe that special angels dwell in the City of Light, each one having uniquely different powers depending on the hero's mission. Perhaps some of these legendary heroes of ancient history were guided by angels from a parallel universe.

It is more likely that heroes such as Huang Ti were guided by a combination of spiritual guides, angels, perhaps aliens, political, military, and religious advisors, and the collective willpower of their people. For when the hero soul experiences a rebirth (the Great Awakening), the entire universe unfolds. Every thing, every person, every being, every intelligent particle in the cosmos cooperates to bring the hero's mission to light.

PEACE

"How wonderful it is that nobody need wait a single moment before starting to improve the world."
– Anne Frank

September 11, 2001 was a day of tragedy that the world will never forget. In possibly the most devastating attack in U.S. history, on American soil, terrorists hijacked four U.S. airliners, and crashed two of the planes into the World Trade Center, one into the Pentagon, and the other just 80 miles southeast of Pittsburgh. The whole world looked on in disbelief as New York's 110-story, twin World Trade towers collapsed into a smoking pile of rubble. The moment was surreal. It felt like an eerie nightmare. But it wasn't a nightmare. A great, collective scream of horror rang out through the world. In the aftermath, a severely wounded nation, and countries all over the world, mourned the loss of thousands of innocent lives from every race, creed, and color.

All of a sudden, America's problem became everyone's problem, for the financial capital of the world had taken a severe blow. People whose lives were shaken around the globe asked 'Why?' Why did this happen? Why is there so much hate against America? These questions will haunt our minds for years to come. I don't think anyone will ever fully know the answers.

Although I don't believe that anyone who is innocent deserves tragedy, I also don't believe that bad things just happen. I believe the horrors we experience in life are but reflections of our own distorted egos. For many years, America had enjoyed an unprecedented financial surplus, while at the same time, ran up a massive spiritual deficit.

The spiritual Pledge of Allegiance to the flag of the United States of America, officially recognized by the U.S.

Congress, states: "I Pledge Allegiance to the flag of the United States of America and to the Republic for which it stands, one Nation under God, indivisible, with liberty and justice for all." Yet politically correct politicians conveniently left out the words, *'under God.'* Every American dollar bill cries out, "In God We Trust." Yet God quickly became a dirty word reserved for the Bible Belt, right-wing Republicans, and church pews. Mass conformity to Commercialism became the demigod of the nation.

I believe America, over the years, developed a giant EGO as the world's only super power. Motivational speaker and author, Les Brown, calls it 'Edging God Out.' The American people, corporately as a nation, had forgotten the Divinity which dwells in every being around the world. New York, the financial capital of the world, with its dark, bleeding, hollowed-out, ruinous eye pits, was but an outward symbol of America's lost soul. America lost touch with her soul many years ago, and with it, the universal spiritual values that sustain peace.

Martin Luther King, Jr. warned America and the world of this imbalance when he declared, "Our scientific power has out run our spiritual power. We have guided missiles and misguided men." Balance had to be restored.

Even before Dr. King, it was Mahatma Gandhi, the great Indian spiritual leader who defied the British Empire and freed his country through the principles of peace and nonviolence (spiritual principles that inspired many great Freedom Fighters including Martin Luther King Jr., Nelson Mandela, Daisaku Ikeda, and the Dalai Lama), who prophetically said, "The things that will destroy us are: politics without principle; pleasure without conscience; wealth without work; knowledge without character; business without morality; science without humanity, and worship without sacrifice." Balance had to be restored.

Sadly, it took a tragedy of such immense proportions to corporately unite a nation in prayer and sing, "God Bless America." In the midst of such devastation, in some strange and mysterious way that cannot be explained, the faith of Americans was strengthened and renewed. It has been said that there are no atheists in a foxhole. But must we wait for another tragedy to realize the lesson that to be truly human means to connect mind with spirit? Have we not learned that there is so much unnecessary illness and hatred in the world because our divine soul has been disconnected? How can one have respect and compassion for others when one cannot even see the Divinity within oneself? Perhaps these are the questions that America, and the world, should be asking.

One encouraging thing that happened from the aftermath of September 11 is that America did not break from the blow of terror, but instead, grew even stronger in spirit. New York City Mayor, Rudolph Giuliani, symbolized this lionesque strength by boldly rallying his people together in a great time of need. He renewed hope in the nation when he defiantly proclaimed, "Hatred, prejudice, and anger are what caused this terrible tragedy, and the people of the City of New York should act differently. We should act bravely. We should act in a tolerant way. We should go about our business, and we should show these people that they can't stop us."

A hero emerged from the wake of the disaster. In London, the Queen awarded Rudolph Giuliani an honorary knighthood at Buckingham Palace for his leadership role. Even though Giuliani became a 'Knight of the British Empire,' he dedicated his title to the real heroes – the people of New York.

Ed Fine's dust-covered image, showing him walking through a cloud of debris holding a paper towel held over his mouth and nose while still clasping on to his briefcase, became an icon of 'the indomitable spirit of the American businessman.' He was one of the lucky few who escaped unscathed. Having attended a meeting on the 87th floor of the North Tower of the World Trade Center, he was on his way down waiting to change elevators on the 78th floor when one of the jets flew into the building. Not knowing what had happened, Mr. Fine started making his way down one of the staircases as the building started to fill with smoke.

By the time he emerged from the building, the street was strewn with burning wreckage and the bodies of people who had jumped from the flaming tower. As he got out, the building immediately started to collapse in a 'colossal cloud of smoke and debris.' His life was surprisingly spared. He now believes he was saved for a reason. His life will never be the same.

Mr. Fine candidly recalled 'that as he prepared for bed at his home in North Plainfield on the night of Sept. 11, he looked out his window and saw a huge buck deer lying on his lawn. The deer turned and stared at him.'

"It was like I was looking into God's eyes," he said. "And He was looking into my soul. He was saying to me, 'If you thought you were alone, you weren't. I was with you every step of the way.'" [Taken from *The Globe and Mail*, March 11, 2002, *World Section*] Reading this article at the time brought instant tears to my eyes. The truth hit home – hard.

On March 11, 2002, to strains of "America the Beautiful," two bright pillars of light beamed out into the night sky, emerging from the dark ashes of ground zero as a Tribute in Light in memory of the lives lost in the September 11 attacks. The beams of light represented much more than the fallen towers of the World Trade Center. The twin towers of light symbolized a new hope and the resiliency and triumph of the human spirit. We can all learn from this experience to better ourselves and the world around us.

Business, political, and religious leaders now have a very important role to play and must become more visible to serve as role models of excellence while honoring their word. Upon his second-term victory, British Prime Minister, Tony Blair, stated, "We can have a politics in which head and heart are married together, in which ambition and compassion lie easily with one another." It is our duty to hold leaders accountable for what they say and take them to task if their words ring hollow. And it is our own responsibility to bring the soul back into business and politics, to humanize the corporate machine, and to balance ambition for profits with compassion for people. We can't wait for another tragedy to learn this lesson.

Today, every corporation has a financial statement. Every corporation should also have a compassion statement measuring performance in corporate responsibility, in providing opportunities to the less fortunate, in using profits responsibly, in giving and charity, in building and improving their communities, in environmental friendliness, in providing education and leadership for youth, in retaining and respecting the elderly, and in humanizing the workforce.

Acclaimed actor, academy award winning Director and Producer, Robert Redford, exemplifies this spirit of responsible leadership and earned a citation in Time Magazine's "25 Most Influential People" in '96. The Academy of Motion Picture Arts and Sciences paid tribute to Mr. Redford's enormous contributions to the motion picture industry by awarding him an Honorary Oscar for a lifetime of achievement at the 74th Annual Academy Awards.

But Mr. Redford's character transcends Hollywood and goes well beyond this award. For over twenty years since his founding of the non-profit, the Sundance Institute, this man has dedicated his time and efforts in giving back to the community by supporting new independent filmmakers and nurturing creative freedom and diversity. Notwithstanding this, Robert Redford is also a highly visible environmental activist who has demonstrated deep reverence for our Mother Earth and the well-being of her people.

Mr. Redford had the courage to voice what we are all responsible for when he said, "We've poisoned the air, the water, and the land. In our passion to control nature, things have gone out of control. Progress from now on has to mean something different. We're running out of resources and we are running out of time."

Does the world need more heroes? Yes. Absolutely, yes! Charles Darwin's era of 'evolution' may be over. We are no longer evolving in the broadest sense of the term. Looking at the same mistakes that humanity keeps repeating throughout history, it seems as if we are in a stage of de-evolution and descension. The scientific community labels our race as belonging to the *Homo sapiens* ("Man, the wise" in Latin) species. How can this be true? How can we be so arrogant to call ourselves 'wise?' How can we be an 'intelligent' species, when we are killing each other and destroying and polluting our Mother Earth? How can we be 'evolving' when parents are killing their children, when children are killing their parents, and when millions of our own people lie starving and destitute? The new race that emerges from our ashes will look at our extinct species, having lasted but a few seconds in the cosmic year of earth's creation, through the glass window of a museum and say to their children, "Those were The Barbarians of the 21st Century."

Evil has its limit. We have reached that limit. If we do not reverse our path of destruction, our children, and our children's children, will cry blood tears, and we will drown in our own sea of ruin. The hero's task will require a tremendous conscious effort to reverse this path and destroy our collective ego. In order to accomplish this, the hero must learn to become humble and aware. With humility comes wisdom and great power. With great power comes great responsibility.

It's our heroes' responsibility to share their knowledge; to teach people to be their own leaders and fight the 'holy war' *inside*, the war between light and the forces of darkness. They must teach us how to destroy the legion of demons that lie within us. Heroes must lead by example and operate from wisdom, love, and compassion. Their purpose is to help annihilate the ego and achieve liberation of the soul. This is the great 'Revolution of the Soul.'

Kahlil Gibran, Lebanese poet, philosopher, and artist, in his landmark book, *The Prophet*, gave humanity the following words of wisdom: " ...And before you leave the marketplace, see that no one has gone his way with empty hands. For the master spirit of the earth shall not sleep peacefully upon the wind till the needs of the least of you are satisfied." In other words, we are only as strong as the weakest link in the marketplace. And the marketplace is no longer the sole domain of America and Europe. The marketplace is the world. The marketplace includes 'half of the world population that lives in poverty (Mats Karlsson, World Bank Group).' Only by lifting up the poor and the weak can we become stronger.

I often spend many hours to choose very carefully the quotes at the beginning of every chapter, because a great quote inspires and succinctly captures the essence of the message I want to convey in that chapter. For the message of peace, I did not choose a deep, sophisticated, and poetic quote, requiring much thought.

Instead, I chose the words of adorable hero-sweetheart, Anne Frank, who at the tender age of thirteen went into hiding from the Nazis in Amsterdam during World War II. Her only 'crime' was being a Jew. Anne Frank's simple innocence and big soul touched the hearts of millions around the world as she documented her feelings and thoughts on war and the struggle to maintain some form of normalcy as a young, adolescent girl in a war-torn country. Her message is simple and immediately doable, "How wonderful it is that nobody need wait a single moment before starting to improve the world."

Nobody need wait. We can all start, now, to improve the world, in our own small and humble way. Perhaps the best way we can do that is by improving ourselves first. Daisaku Ikeda, a distinguished Buddhist philosopher, poet, peace leader, and founder and President of Soka Gakkai International (a Buddhist organization with over 12 million members worldwide), once said, "A great revolution in just one single individual will help achieve a change in the destiny of a society and, further, will enable a change in the destiny of humankind." Recipient of over fifty honorary doctorates, and over 170 awards and citations from cities around the world, including the 1999 World Citizenship Award presented by the Nuclear Age Peace Foundation and the 1983 U.N. Peace Medal, Daisaku Ikeda is our modern day Prince of Peace.

Start by changing yourself first, making yourself a better person – a more compassionate, caring, and loving human being. Become a responsible world citizen, a warrior of peace, and the world will expand and respond in likeness. Start, as Gandhi once said, "by being the change you wish to see."

CITIZENS OF ETERNITY

"Be absolute for death; for either death or life shall be the sweeter."
– Shakespeare

Many people today believe that what they are is the human machine and that the mysterious spirit just happens to vaguely dwell somewhere within that machine. This is why there is much illness and suffering in the world. People are not able to break free from their own personal limitations of themselves because their existing level of thinking holds them prisoners.

We are majestic kings and queens, soaring high over mountains - the skies and heavens above our true dwelling place. We are great spiritual beings having a human experience, and not the other way around. I am not afraid of physical death, because I believe that our bodies are but articles of clothing for the soul, to be eventually discarded for a new garment.

Here is a divine truth for the hero soul to reflect on:

"All things are in process, rising and returning. Plants come to blossom, but only to return to the root. Returning to the root is like seeking tranquility. Seeking tranquility is like moving toward destiny. To move toward destiny is like eternity. To know eternity is enlightenment, and not to recognize eternity brings disorder and evil. Knowing eternity makes one comprehensive; comprehension makes one broadminded; breadth of vision brings nobility; nobility is like heaven. The heaven is like Tao. Tao is the Eternal. The decay of the body is not to be feared."
– Lao Tse, *Tao Teh Ching*, 604 B.C.

Norman Vincent Peale, the man who brought the power of positive thinking movement to the forefront and spiritually enlightened millions of people around the world, is a great hero in my book. After reading his most famous work, *The Power of Positive Thinking*, I'm convinced Dr. Peale had subtle knowledge of the mysteries of the eternal and communicated the boon of such wisdom in simple ways that people could understand and apply.

In his international bestseller, *The Power of Positive Thinking,* Dr. Peale writes, "Of these deep and tender matters I personally have no doubt whatsoever. I firmly believe in the continuation of life after that which we call death takes place. I believe there are two sides to the phenomenon known as death – this side where we now live and the other side where we shall continue to live. Eternity does not start with death. We are in eternity now. We are citizens of eternity. We merely change the form of the experience called life, and that change, I am persuaded, is for the better."

He goes on to say, "The late Mrs. Thomas A. Edison told me that when her famous husband was dying, he whispered to his physician, 'It is beautiful over there.' Edison was the world's greatest scientist. All his life he had worked with phenomena. He was of a factual cast of mind. He never reported anything as a fact until he saw it work. He would never have reported, 'It is very beautiful over there' unless, having seen, he knew it to be true."

When death smiles on you, smile back; for death is beautiful. Heroes proudly wear the crown of death. They search the faces of the gods and know the eternal spirit. In their wisdom they come to know that there is an awesome Higher Power. They know that we are not alone, and that this spirit is a guiding light in our lives. There is a God that listens, that cares, that responds to our deepest desires. The divine soul is in all of us.

In knowing this, the hero soul treats everyone with deep and profound respect. Heroes cannot take with them their material possessions to the grave. What they will be remembered for is not what they have taken, but what they have given. They give of everything they have, leaving a great legacy behind. And people love them for it.

When Pierre Elliot Trudeau, the great Canadian Prime Minister, the man who defined the soul of modern Canada, passed away, his son, Justin Trudeau, honored him. In closing his stirring eulogy, Justin spoke dearly and passionately about his father: "He won't be coming back anymore. It's all up to us, all of us, now. The woods are lovely, dark and deep. He has kept his promises and earned his sleep. Je t'aime, papa."

Thousands upon thousands of mourners, from all over the world, lined up at Parliament Hill in Ottawa to pay their respects to a great man who left a great legacy behind.

Have we earned our sleep? Are you prepared to wear the crown of death? What act will you play on the stage of life? A hero, a villain, or nothing? What concept do you have of your self? Will your deeds have a positive impact on people's lives? Will you leave behind a legacy that will be honored? Will the great halls of life reverberate with your unique voice - echoing through eternity? Think of these things, my dear, beloved readers, and act, before out life's brief candle.

> **"All the world's a stage,**
> **And all the men and women merely players;**
> **They have their exits and their entrances;**
> **And one man in his time plays many parts,**
> **His acts being seven ages."**
>
> **– William Shakespeare,** *As You Like It*

EPILOGUE

"Our deepest fear is not that we are inadequate. Our deepest fear is that we are powerful beyond measure. It is our light, not our darkness that most frightens us. We ask ourselves, 'who am I to be brilliant, gorgeous, talented, and fabulous?' Actually, who are we not to be? You are a child of God. Your playing small does not serve the world. There is nothing so enlightening about shrinking so that other people won't feel insecure around you. We are born to make manifest the glory of God which is within us. It is not in just some of us. It is in all of us. And as we let our own light shine, we unconsciously give other people permission to do the same. As we are liberated from our own fears, our presence automatically liberates others."

– Marianne Williamson

For some of you, this will be the end of the beginning; the message buried deep in the shadows and dust of distant memory, never to be experienced again. But for those of you who have taken the message to heart and consciously chosen the way of the hero, it is only the beginning. What next?

Like a lion in the desert, you must carve out your own path and take the road less traveled. Following the status quo will only lead to a path of mediocrity. Regardless of what other people are telling you to do on the contrary, follow your bliss and do your own thing.

Even if everyone around you has stopped believing in you, you must never stop believing in your dream. Keep the faith. For faith and fear cannot exist together. When you dig deep within yourself and discover the hero within, you will awaken the hero soul, and reconnect with the Spirit. And fear vanishes in the presence of Spirit because it has no fear – it is pure love. Unlike the ego, the Spirit is not afraid of death, because it is immortal; it will never die because it was never born. Life and death are merely changes of clothing in the wardrobe of the soul.

And so, do not be afraid. Do not hold back. Let your light shine brightly unto the world. Put your talents to use and pursue your endeavors with all your might and power. But do it responsibly. Be a responsible world citizen dedicated to promoting peace and prosperity in the world.

The time for looting the masses, plundering our valuable natural resources, polluting the environment, killing each other, and raping the earth is soon coming to an end. Ambition and compassion *must* coexist together harmoniously. There is no other way if we are to provide a better future for ourselves and our children.

While the scientific debate rages on as to the causes of phenomena such as global warming, an imminent global catastrophe is at hand, as *tens of thousands* of people die each year due to air pollution caused mainly from the burning of fossil fuels. And this same toxic soot which is killing us is also contributing to global warming which threatens to destroy over one quarter of the world's plants and animals. We are destroying ourselves and these beautiful creatures responsible for sustaining the earth and maintaining equilibrium, as a result of our *own* folly! If we do not change and learn to cooperate with nature, we will eventually be wiped off the face of the earth.

This global warming is the 'high fever' of mother earth. Instead of being positive bacteria to rejuvenate life, we have become a nasty virus. When you get a virus you get the fever which cooks your blood. That is what is happening to us. Imagine your skin being bombed millions of times by tiny little bombs, like a horde of mosquitoes biting into your flesh and sucking your blood. How long could you tolerate such pain? Wouldn't you eventually wipe out these 'pests'?

Isn't that what warring humankind is doing dropping thousands of bombs every day on the mountains, the land, the trees, dumping waste in the ocean, spewing soot in the air? The earth is one gigantic living organism, and we have become like fleas on its skin – to be wiped off. The fire, the fever, is mother earth purifying itself.

The hero's path requires responsibility towards the earth, towards humanity, and towards divinity. Indeed, 'progress from now on has to mean something different.' In order to redeem ourselves, we must change. By honoring the Divine in all things, we honor ourselves.

You can begin living a victorious life by creating wealth responsibly, by giving back to the community, by sharing your wealth, and by supporting causes that are dedicated to protecting the environment, promoting peace, and helping people to prosper in a responsible way.

Do not remain silent when you encounter injustice. Speak out against wrongdoing and malfeasance. Saying no to the oppressor dignifies both the oppressor and the oppressed, for it teaches respect, which is the foundation of love.

Now go out into the world and live your dreams with passion! Do not be discouraged or dismayed. After much toil, sweat, blood, and tears, you will still encounter failure along the way. Your spirit and strength will be tested by life to see if you have what it takes to enter the circle of herohood. Persist and persevere for victory belongs to those who want it the most and stay in it the longest.

You will find, as a general rule of thumb, that most people prefer to back a winner over a loser. We've all seen this principle in action. Banks lend money to people who don't need it. Wealthy patrons often support individuals and organizations that already have lots of backing and financial support. Everybody wants a winner. Nobody wants a loser.

So what's the lesson? Be a winner! Persist, persevere, keep on keeping on. You'll be surprised to see how many people come out of the wood works to support you because they realize you're here to stay and are not going away.

Never, ever, give up on your dreams! Even for one brief, fleeting moment where you own your dream and hold it to your heart is worth more than a thousand lifetimes lived in mediocrity. It is better to die for freedom, than live for nothing. The freedom to live your dreams.

What have you got to lose to start living your dreams now? You have nothing to lose but your precious life, which is already dead without a dream. To paraphrase Shakespeare, "A coward dies a thousand deaths; the valiant die but once." What have you got to lose? Are you willing to commit to your dreams, as death commits to life?

If the answer is yes, then begin at once by being who you were born to be. Use your talents in pursuit of a worthy ideal. Give of yourself and live each precious moment on purpose, in service to others. For the greatest reward goes to those who render the greatest service.

"Soul is where man ends, and eternity begins."
- Sharif Khan

For inspirational keynotes, seminars, and workshops that will entertain, educate, and empower, contact Sharif at:

Diamond Mind Enterprises
c/o Sharif N. Khan
35 Douville Court
Toronto, Ontario M5A 4E7 Canada
Phone: (416) 417-1259
Email: **sharif@herosoul.com**

www.HeroSoul.com

**SPONSORSHIP OPPORTUNITIES ARE AVAILABLE FOR
SELECT GROUPS FOSTERING RESPONSIBLE LEADERSHIP**

PSYCHOLOGY
OF THE
HERO SOUL

SHARIF N. KHAN

QUICK ORDER FORM

To order more copies send check or money order payable to Diamond Mind Enterprises:

Diamond Mind Enterprises
c/o Sharif Khan
35 Douville Court
Toronto, Ontario M5A 4E7
416-417-1259
sharif@herosoul.com
www.herosoul.com

PSYCHOLOGY OF THE HERO SOUL
SHARIF N. KHAN
ISBN 0-9731922-0-8 / $ 19.95 CDN / $ 14.95 US

Please send me _____ copies of *Psychology of the Hero Soul.*

$_____ **Subtotal**
$_____ Shipping
$_____ Taxes
$_____ **Total enclosed**

SHIPPING in Canada: add $5 for first book and $1 for each additional book. **US:** add $10 for first book and $2 for each additional book. **International:** add $20 for first book and $4 for each additional book.
TAXES: Canadian residents, add 7% GST
                              SHIP TO:
Name:_____
Street Address:_____
City:_____Province/State:_____
Postal/Zip_____Country:_____
E-Mail Address:_____
Phone Number:(_____) _____
☐ **Yes,** please subscribe me to the FREE monthly Hero Soul eZine. I have provided my email address above.